General Knowledge Olympiad

Class 08

A must have book for all
Olympiads & Talent Search Exams...

by
Reena Kar

BLoOM CAP
Bloom Cap Edu Ventures Pvt. Ltd.

Bloom Cap Edu Ventures Pvt. Ltd.

卐 **Administrative & Production Office**

'Ramchhaya' 4577/15, Agarwal Road, Darya Ganj, New Delhi -110002
Tele: 011- 47630600, 43518550

卐 **ISBN :** 978-93-25519-47-3

卐 **PRICE :** ₹100.00

卐 **PO No :** TXT-XX-XXXXXXX-X-XX

For further information about the books log on to
www.bloomcap.org

Follow us on   

Preface

"Future belongs to those Who prepares for it today"

School Olympiads are National & International level competitions conducted by different Government, Non-Government & Educational Organisations with the purpose of making the children ready to face competitive exams. The challenging Questions asked in Olympiads motivate them to learn more & more and bring out the best result with improved academic performance. The Awards & Scholarship offered by Olympiads motivate children to aspire & strive for doing better and emerge out to be the best.

GK Olympiads

GK is the knowledge of every aspect of the human life, which may or may not be the part of routine academic studies but very important for the overall personality development of the students. It is more or less connected with the attentiveness and awareness. There can be different domains of GK like; History, Geography, Polity, Culture, Discovery, Sports, Current Affairs etc.

GK Olympiads help students in understanding the importance of General Knowledge and updations about National & International Affairs in daily life.

'Bloom GK Olympiad Study Book Class 8' is a perfect resource to Study & Practice for Olympiad Exams and other National & State Level Talent Search Exams & Other Competitions.

Some Special Features of Bloom GK Olympiad Study Books are;

- Complete coverage of all the topics related to GK;. History, Geography, Environment, Polity, Science, Sports, etc.
- Chapterwise Exercises having different types of Objective Questions.
- Olympiad Pattern Practice Sets at the end.

This book is prepared by Expert Panel with the utmost care, still if you have any suggestions regarding its improvement then feel free to contact us at olympiads@bloomcap.org. We will try to inculcate your suggestions in the further editions.

Contents

Introduction to European Power

1 Mark Questions

1. Who discovered a sea route to India in 1498?
   (a) Ralph Fitch
   (b) Thomas Cook
   (c) Vasco da Gama
   (d) Christopher Columbus

2. Who was the Nawab of Bengal at the time of Battle of Plassey ?
   (a) Sirajuddaulah
   (b) Alivardi Khan
   (c) Murshid Quli Khan
   (d) Tipu Sultan

3. The English Army commander who defeated the Nawab of Bengal in the Battle of Plassey was ....
   (a) Robert Clive   (b) Thomas Reed
   (c) Hector Munro   (d) Lord Wellesley

4. Tipu Sultan was the famous ruler of ....
   (a) Awadh   (b) Mysore
   (c) Bengal   (d) Punjab

5. Who among the following didn't fight the Battle of Buxar from Indian side?
   (a) Tipu Sultan   (b) Shujauddaulah
   (c) Sirajuddaulah   (d) Shah Alam

6. Which of the following Governer General introduced the policy of 'Doctrine of Lapse'?
   (a) Lord Dalhousie (b) Lord Hasting
   (c) Lord Cornwallis (d) Robert Clive

7. Which of the following was the first European power to reach India?
   (a) British   (b) Portuguese
   (c) Ireland   (d) Scotland

8. Which one of the following European powers supported 'Tipu Sultan' in his war efforts with the Britishers?
   (a) Portuguese   (b) French
   (c) Dutch   (d) Spanish

9. The British conquest of Bengal began with the Battle of ....
   (a) Buxar   (b) Seringapatam
   (c) Panipat   (d) Plassey

10. Which of the following British Queens were given the title of Empress of India during British period?
    (a) Queen Elizabeth
    (b) Queen Mary
    (c) Queen Victoria
    (d) Queen Anne

11. Who among the following became the Nawab of Bengal after the Battle of Plassey?
    (a) Mir Jafar   (b) Mir Qasim
    (c) Mir Jumla   (d) Sirajuddaulah

12. Which one of the following crops was introduced by the Portuguese in India?
    (a) Opium   (b) Coffee
    (c) Betal leaf   (d) Chilli

13. What is the name of the fort constructed by British in Calcutta?
    (a) Fort Saint David
    (b) Fort Saint Andrew
    (c) Fort William
    (d) Fort Victoria

14. The English established their first factory in India at ………. .
    (a) Bombay   (b) Surat
    (c) Sutanuti   (d) Madras

2 Marks Questions

15. Which of the following statement is correct?
    1. The English East India Company was granted permission by Mughal rulers to trade with India.
    2. The English East India Company was the first company to be setup in India.

    Codes
    (a) Only 1   (b) Only 2
    (c) Both 1 and 2   (d) None of these

16. Which of the following pair is not correctly matched?
    (a) Bahadur Shah Zafar – Last Mughal Emperor
    (b) Robert Clive – First Governor of Bihar
    (c) Mir Jafar – Nawab of Bengal
    (d) Ranjit Singh – Maharaja of Gwalior

17. Match the following.

Europeans	Base in India
A. Portuguese	1. Goa
B. French	2. Pondicherry
C. English	3. Calcutta

Codes

	A	B	C
(a)	2	1	3
(b)	1	2	3
(c)	3	2	1
(d)	3	1	2

18. Which among the following is a correct chronology of arrival of European Powers in India?
    (a) Portuguese, British, French, Dutch
    (b) French, Dutch, British, Portuguese
    (c) Portuguese, British, Dutch, French
    (d) French, British, Portuguese, Dutch

19. Which of the following statements is/are correct?
    1. Jahangir was the Mughal Emperor when British first came to India.
    2. The British first arrived at port of Pondicherry.

    Codes
    (a) Only 1
    (b) Only 2
    (c) Both 1 and 2
    (d) None of the above

Tribal Movement

1 Mark Questions

1. Birsa Munda led the tribal movement in
   ....
   (a) Chota Nagpur region
   (b) Satpura region
   (c) Central Province
   (d) Himalayan region

2. What was the other name of shifting cultivation practiced by the tribals in India?
   (a) Padhua Cultivation
   (b) Bedia Cultivation
   (c) Jhoom Cultivation
   (d) None of the above

3. What was the main occupation of Khond tribe of Odisha?
   (a) Settled cultivation
   (b) Nomadic herding
   (c) Fishing
   (d) Hunting-gathering

4. The Gaddi tribes of Kulla region were mostly......... .
   (a) Cultivators   (b) Hunters
   (c) Shepherds   (d) Food gatherers

5. Which of the following tribal groups was/ware engaged in settled cultivation?
   (a) Santhal
   (b) Gond
   (c) Both (a) and (b)
   (d) Khond

6. Which among the following is incorrectly matched?
   (a) Kols-Chota Nagpur
   (b) Ahom-Assam
   (c) Kuka Movement-Kerala
   (d) D. Khasi uprising-Garo and Jaintia hills

7. Which of the following tribal groups was/were seen as civilised by the Britishers?
   (a) Gond and Santhal (b) Khond
   (c) Baiga   (d) Naga

8. Which of the following tribal leader was considered as 'Bhagavan' by his followers?
   (a) Sidhu   (b) Kanhu
   (c) Birsa Munda   (d) Veer Narain

9. Which of the following tribal groups was engaged in the rearing of cocoon?
   (a) Khond   (b) Bhil
   (c) Santhal   (d) Gaddi

10. The Gaddi tribe of Himachal Pradesh practised which of the following activity?
    (a) Shifting Cultivation
    (b) Animal Rearing
    (c) Horticulture
    (d) Jhum Cultivation

11. Santhal revolt (1855-56) was led by ....
(a) Siddhu-Kanhu
(b) Chand-Bhairav
(c) Both (a) and (b)
(d) Neither (a) nor (b)

12. Which of the following is not tribal movement?
(a) Tebhaga Movement
(b) Chuars Movement
(c) Bhils Movement
(d) Kolis Movement

13. Birsa Munda founded which of the following religion?
(a) Vaishnav   (b) Khorayat
(c) Birsait   (d) Adivaraha

14. What was the main region of Ho revolt which was started in 1820-21?
(a) Chota Nagpur   (b) Bhagalpur
(c) Haryana   (d) Punjab

15. Tribals were recruited in large numbers in tea gardens of ....
(a) Tamil Nadu   (b) Assam
(c) Karnataka   (d) Odisha

16. Which tribe was popular for silk rearing?
(a) Bhils   (b) Gonds
(c) Santhals   (d) Paikas

17. Tribals were recruited in large numbers in coal mines of ....
(a) Bihar   (b) Maharashtra
(c) Madhya Pradesh (d) Tamil Nadu

2 Marks Questions

18. Consider the following statements regarding tribal revolts.
1. Tribal revolts were led by members who come from outside the tribal society.
2. It was against the British colonial authorities and the groups supported by British.

Which of the statements given above is/are correct?

(a) Only 1
(b) Only 2
(c) Both 1 and 2
(d) None of the above

19. Which of the following pairs (tribal revolts and their leaders) is not correct?
(a) Santhal Revolt-Siddhu and Kanhu
(b) Munda Revolt-Birsa Munda
(c) Ramosi uprising-Chittu Singh
(d) Khond Uprising-Vinoba Bhave

20. Match the following.

List I (Tribal Group)	List II (Associated With)
A. Khonds	1. Hunting-gathering
B. Labadis	2. Cattle herding
C. Bakrawal	3. Rearing of goats
D. Santhal	4. Settled agriculture

Codes

	A	B	C	D		A	B	C	D
(a)	1	2	3	4	(b)	2	3	4	1
(c)	2	4	1	3	(d)	3	1	4	3

21. Which of the following statement is true?
1. Gond and Santhals are civilised by Britishers.
2. Birsa Munda led the tribal movements in Chota Nagpur region.

Codes
(a) Only 1   (b) Only 2
(c) Both 1 and 2   (d) None of these

Revolt of 1857

1 Mark Questions

1. Which of the following had started the revolt of 1857?
   (a) Sepoys
   (b) Zamindars
   (c) Peasants
   (d) Plantation workers

2. Mangal Pandey revolted at ....
   (a) Barrackpore   (b) Kanpur
   (c) Meerut   (d) Delhi

3. Who was the Governor-General of India during the revolt of 1857?
   (a) Lord Dalhousie   (b) Lord Canning
   (c) Lord Minto   (d) Lord Bentinck

4. Begum Hazrat Mahal was the leader of revolt in ....
   (a) Kanpur   (b) Delhi
   (c) Lucknow   (d) Jhansi

5. The revolt of 1857 started on ....
   (a) 10th May, 1857
   (b) 14th November, 1857
   (c) 24th March, 1857
   (d) 6th June, 1857

6. Which among the following was the symbol of revolt of 1857?
   (a) Charkha and Khadi cloth
   (b) Lotus and Chapati (Bread)
   (c) Rose and Hat
   (d) Sword and Wheat Bran

7. The largest number of soldiers who participated in the struggle of 1857 came from ....
   (a) Bengal   (b) Bihar
   (c) Awadh   (d) Rajasthan

8. Who among the following led the sepoys at Kanpur in the 1857 uprising?
   (a) Tatya Tope
   (b) Rani Lakshmibai
   (c) Nana Saheb
   (d) Kunwar Singh

9. Who led the 1857 revolt in Bihar?
   (a) Babu Kunwar Singh
   (b) Hare Krishna Singh
   (c) Amar Singh
   (d) Raja Shahzada Singh

10. The 1857 revolt began from which of the following city?
    (a) Delhi   (b) Lucknow
    (c) Meerut   (d) Lahore

11. After the suppression of revolt, Britishers imprisoned Bahadur Shah Zafar in ....
    (a) Rangoon   (b) Delhi
    (c) Calcutta   (d) Nepal

12. Rani Avantibai Lodhi was leader of revolt in......... .
    (a) Jhansi   (b) Punjab
    (c) Ramgarh   (d) Pune

13. During the revolt of 1857, the term 'Firangis' denotes ....
   (a) Britishers　　(b) Zamindar
   (c) Tribal people　(d) None of these

14. Who among the following was proclaimed by the rebels all over the country as the leader of revolt of 1857?
   (a) Nana Saheb
   (b) Kunwar Singh
   (c) Bahadur Shah Zafar
   (d) Bakht Khan

15. Rani Lakshmibai was the leader of the revolt in ....
   (a) Jhansi
   (b) Benaras
   (c) Lucknow
   (d) Delhi

16. Who among the following was not associated with the revolt of 1857?
   (a) Tatya Tope
   (b) Rani Lakshmibai
   (c) Bahadur Shah Zafar
   (d) Bhagat Singh

17. The powers of the East India Company was transferred to British Crown in ....
   (a) 1857　　　(b) 1858
   (c) 1856　　　(d) 1813

18. After suppression of revolt of 1857, Britishers recruited large number of soldiers from which of the following communities?
   (a) Gurkhas　　(b) Sikhs
   (c) Pathans　　(d) All of these

2 Marks Questions

19. Which of the following were the religious causes of revolt of 1857?
   1. Introduction of greased cartridges
   2. Free hand to the Christian missionaries
   3. Abolishment of Sati

   Which of the statements given above are correct?
   (a) Only 1 and 2　(b) Only 2 and 3
   (c) Only 1 and 3　(d) All of these

20. Match the following.

Leaders of Revolt		Regions
A. Rani Lakshmibai		1. Jhansi
B. Tatya Tope		2. Kanpur
C. Begum Hazrat Mahal		3. Bihar
D. Kunwar Singh		4. Lucknow

Codes

	A	B	C	D		A	B	C	D
(a)	1	2	3	4	(b)	1	2	4	3
(c)	2	4	1	3	(d)	3	1	4	3

21. Match the following.

Leaders	Areas under their Operation
A. Kunwar Singh	1. Barrackpore
B. Mangal Pandey	2. Jagdishpur
C. Bakht Khan	3. Kanpur
D. Nana Saheb	4. Delhi

Codes

	A	B	C	D		A	B	C	D
(a)	1	2	3	4	(b)	4	3	1	2
(c)	2	1	4	3	(d)	3	1	4	3

Women, Caste and Reforms

1 Mark Questions

1. The Brahmo Samaj was founded by ....
   (a) Dayanand Saraswati
   (b) Raja Ram Mohan Roy
   (c) Jyotiba Phule
   (d) B.R. Ambedkar

2. The Asiatic Society of Bengal was established by......... .
   (a) Thomas Macaulay
   (b) Richard Wellesely
   (c) Charles Metcalf
   (d) William Jones

3. Wood's dispatch presented in 1850s was related to ....
   (a) Revenue
   (b) Education
   (c) Land Reform
   (d) Irrigation Reform

4. The first society founded by Raja Ram Mohan Roy was ....
   (a) BrahmoSamaj
   (b) Atmiya Sabha
   (c) Brahmo Sabha
   (d) Tattwabodhini Sabha

5. Satya Shodak Samaj was established by ....
   (a) Jyotiba Phule
   (b) Raja Ram Mohan Roy
   (c) Ishwar Chandra Vidyasagar
   (d) B.R. Ambedkar

6. Brahmo Samaj was founded in the Year of ....
   (a) 1827 (b) 1829 (c) 1828 (d) 1830

7. The first women's school was started by who among the following?
   (a) Dayanand Saraswati
   (b) Jyotibha Phule
   (c) Ishwar Chandra Vidyasagar
   (d) None of the above

8. The organisation established by the Dayanand Saraswati was ....
   (a) Brahmo Samaj   (b) Arya Samaj
   (c) Prarthana Samaj (d) Bahujan Samaj

9. In which of the following years, the evil practice of Sati was banned?
   (a) 1825   (b) 1856
   (c) 1829   (d) 1858

10. Who among the following played the main role in enactment of Widow Remarriage Act?
- (a) Ishwar Chandra Vidyasagar
- (b) Raja Ram Mohan Roy
- (c) D. K. Karve
- (d) Pandita Ramabai

11. Who among the following formed the association for widow remarriage in Madras Presidency?
- (a) Veerasalingam Pantulu
- (b) Narayan Guru
- (c) C. Rajagopalachari
- (d) N.M. Lokhande

12. Sati practise was banned due to the efforts of which of the following?
- (a) Pandita Ramabai
- (b) Raja Ram Mohan Roy
- (c) Mahatma Gandhi
- (d) Syed Ahmad Khan

13. Who among the following was the author of book named 'Stripurushtulna'?
- (a) Tarabai Shinde
- (b) Pandita Ramabai
- (c) Annie Besant
- (d) None of these

14. Shanti Niketan was started by ....
- (a) Mahatma Gandhi
- (b) Raja Ram Mohan Roy
- (c) Rabindranath Tagore
- (d) Narayan Guru

2 Marks Questions

15. Which of the following pairs is not correctly matched?

	Leaders	Supported
(a)	Swami Dayanand Saraswati	Reforms in Hinduism
(b)	Jyotiba Phule	Eradication of untouchability and system
(c)	Thomas Macaulay	Promotion of education in vernacular language
(d)	Ishwar Chandra Vidyasagar	Widow remarriage

16. Match the following.

	Socio-Religious Reform Movement		Established at
A.	Prathana Samaj	1.	Belur Math
B.	Veda Samaj	2.	Amritsar
C.	Singh Sabha	3.	Madras
D.	Rama Krishna Mission	4.	Poona

Codes

	A	B	C	D		A	B	C	D
(a)	1	2	3	4	(b)	2	3	4	1
(c)	4	3	2	1	(d)	3	1	4	3

17. Match the following.

	Reform Movement		Leaders
A.	Aligarh Movement	1.	Jyotiba Phule
B.	Satya Shodhak Samaj	2.	Syed Ahmad Khan
C.	Brahmo Sabha	3.	EV. Ramaswamy Naicker
D.	Self-Respect Movement	4.	Raja Ram Mohan Roy

Codes

	A	B	C	D		A	B	C	D
(a)	1	2	3	4	(b)	2	1	4	3
(c)	4	3	2	1	(d)	3	1	4	3

Chapter 05

National Movement of India

1 Mark Questions

1. The Indian National Congress was established in ....
   (a) 1857 (b) 1875 (c) 1897 (d) 1885

2. The British official who helped in the establishment of Indian National Congress was ....
   (a) William Adams (b) V. A Smith
   (c) A. O. Hume   (d) William Jones

3. The Ilbert Bill controversy was related to which of the following?
   (a) Education of Indians
   (b) Power of Judges
   (c) Purna Swaraj
   (d) Revolt of 1857

4. Which of the following organisations were established before Indian National Congress?
   (a) Poona Sarvajanik Sabha
   (b) Madras Mahajan Sabha
   (c) Bombay Presidency Association
   (d) All of the above

5. Who among the following was an extremist leader?
   (a) Pherozeshah Mehta
   (b) Gopal Krishna Gokhle
   (c) Satyendranath Tagore
   (d) Bipin Chandra Pal

6. The Partition of Bengal was announced in ....
   (a) 1904 (b) 1906 (c) 1905 (d) 1907

7. The Swadeshi Movement was launched after which of the following events?
   (a) Partition of Bengal
   (b) Salt Satyagraha
   (c) Chauri Chaura incident
   (d) Rowlatt Act

8. Mahatma Gandhi arrived in India in ....
   (a) 1915   (b) 1917
   (c) 1925   (d) 1909

9. Mahatma Gandhi called off the Non-Cooperation Movement after ....
   (a) Kakori train robbery
   (b) Jallianwala Bagh Massacre
   (c) Chauri-Chaura incident
   (d) None of the above

10. The Hindustan Socialist Republican Association (HSRA) was established by ....
    (a) Bhagat Singh
    (b) Bipin Chandra Pal
    (c) C.R. Das
    (d) Subhash Chandra Bose

11. Who among the following wrote 'Poverty and Un-British Rule in India'?
    (a) Pherozeshah Mehta
    (b) M.G. Ranade
    (c) Dadabhai Naoroji
    (d) R.C Dutt

12. Who became the leader of Dandi March after 'Gandhiji' was arrested?
    (a) Jawaharlal Nehru
    (b) Subhash Chandra Bose
    (c) Abbas Tayyibji
    (d) Annie Besant

13. Before, 1905 the province of Bengal included parts of ....
    (a) Bihar   (b) Jharkhand
    (c) Odisha   (d) All of these

14. Who among the following edited the Marathi newspaper 'Kesari'?
    (a) Bal Gangadhar Tilak
    (b) Bipin Chandra Pal
    (c) Pherozeshah Mehta
    (d) V.D Savarkar

15. The All India Muslim League was established in 1906 at ....
    (a) Lucknow   (b) Lahore
    (c) Dacca   (d) Karachi

16. The Khilafat Movement in India was started in ....
    (a) 1919 (b) 1920 (c) 1909 (d) 1918

17. Which of the following pacts was signed by the Congress and Muslim league to work together for representative government in the country?
    (a) Karachi Pact   (b) Poona Pact
    (c) Lucknow Pact   (d) Surat Pact

18. The Natal Congress was established by Mahatma Gandhi in ....
    (a) South Africa   (b) England
    (c) USA   (d) Canada

19. Which of the following Freedom Movements is also known as August Kranti?
    (a) Civil Disobedience Movement
    (b) Quit India Movement
    (c) Non-Cooperation Movement
    (d) Swadeshi Movement

20. Who among the following denounced his Knighthood after the Jallianwala Bagh Massacre?
    (a) Mahatma Gandhi
    (b) Rabindranath Tagore
    (c) Jawaharlal Nehru
    (d) M.A. Jinnah

21. Who among the following was/were leaders of Khilafat Movement?
    (a) Mohammad Ali (b) Shaukat Ali
    (c) Both (a) and (b) (d) Bhagat Singh

22. During the Non-Cooperation Movement, forest satyagraha was launched in ....
    (a) Andhra Pradesh
    (b) Tamil Nadu
    (c) Gujarat
    (d) Bihar

23. Which of the following was the reason for calling off the Non-Cooperation Movement by Gandhiji?
    (a) Chauri-Chaura incident
    (b) Second Round Table Conference
    (c) Gandhiji's arrest
    (d) Pressure from the British Government

24. The famous Salt March was organised by Gandhiji during which National Movement?
    (a) Swadeshi Movement
    (b) Non-Cooperation Movement
    (c) Quit India Movement
    (d) Civil Disobedience Movement

25. Who was the president of Lahore Session of Congress in which resolution of Purna Swaraj was passed by the Congress?
(a) C. R. Das
(b) Subhash Chandra Bose
(c) Jawaharlal Nehru
(d) Rajendra Prasad

26. Who was the first Indian woman to become President of the Indian National Congress?
(a) Annie Besant   (b) Aruna Asaf Ali
(c) Sarojini Naidu   (d) Bina Devi

27. Who among the following referred Mahatma Gandhi as the 'Father of the Nation'?
(a) Subhash Chandra Bose
(b) Jawaharlal Nehru
(c) Bhagat Singh
(d) Chandra Shekhar Azad

28. Who among the following was known as Frontier Gandhi?
(a) Khan Abdul Ghaffar Khan
(b) C Rajagopalachari
(c) Liyaquat Ali
(d) M.D Barakatullah

29. Mahatma Gandhi gave the mantra of 'Do or Die' in which of the following revolutionary events?
(a) Non-Cooperation Movement
(b) Civil Disobedience Movement
(c) Quit India Movement
(d) Champaran Satyagraha

2 Marks Questions

30. Which of the following pairs is not correctly matched?

	Gandhian Movements	Years
(a)	Swadeshi Movement	1939
(b)	Non-Cooperation Movement	1920
(c)	Civil- Disobedience Movement	1930
(d)	Quit India Movement	1942

31. Match the following.

	Personalities		Associated with
A.	Dadabhai Naoroji	1.	Swarajya Party
B.	Motilal Nehru	2.	Khilafat Movement
C.	Shaukat Ali	3.	First Indian Governor General of India
D.	C. Rajagopalachari	4.	Highlighted the Economic Drain of India

Codes

	A	B	C	D		A	B	C	D
(a)	1	2	3	4	(b)	2	1	4	3
(c)	4	1	2	3	(d)	3	1	4	3

32. Match the following.

	Events		Features
A.	Swadeshi Movement	1.	Forest Satyagraha
B.	Non-Cooperation Movement	2.	National Education
C.	Civil Disobedience Movement	3.	Independent Government
D.	Quit India Movement	4.	Dandi March

Codes

	A	B	C	D		A	B	C	D
(a)	1	2	3	4	(b)	2	1	4	3
(c)	4	1	2	3	(d)	3	1	4	3

India After Independence

1 Mark Questions

1. Which of the following was the first state to be formed on linguistic basis after Independence?
   (a) Madhya Pradesh (b) Andhra Pradesh
   (c) Punjab (d) Uttar Pradesh

2. The Bhudan Movement was started by which among the following after India's Independence?
   (a) Sundar Lal Bahuguna
   (b) Vinoba Bhave
   (c) Jyotirao Phule
   (d) None of the above

3. Which of the following state joined the Indian Union without any referendum or military action?
   (a) Junagarh
   (b) Hyderabad
   (c) Jammu and Kashmir
   (d) Baroda

4. The correct meaning of the term 'Franchise' is......... .
   (a) Right to Live (b) Right to Speak
   (c) Right to Vote (d) Right to Freedom

5. The objective resolution in the Constituent Assembly was presented by......... .
   (a) B. R. Ambedkar
   (b) Sardar Vallabhbhai Patel
   (c) Mahatma Gandhi
   (d) Jawaharlal Nehru

6. Which of the following list is not part of the Indian Constitution, defining the powers of centre and states?
   (a) Union List (b) State List
   (c) Federal List (d) Concurrent List

7. After India's Independence, the Constitution makers adopted the political systems of ....
   (a) Britain (b) USA
   (c) Russia (d) France

8. After the commencement of the Constitution, India adopted the Universal adult franchise granting all Indian above the age of .... ,the right to vote in state and national elections.
   (a) 18 years (b) 21 years
   (c) 16 years (d) 25 years

9. Who became the first President of India after the Independence?
   (a) B. R. Ambedkar
   (b) Sardar Vallabhbhai Patel
   (c) Rajendra Prasad
   (d) Jawaharlal Nehru

10. The first Nuclear Test of India, after Independence was code named as ....
    (a) Shakti
    (b) Smiling Buddha
    (c) Pokhran
    (d) Rohini

11. What was the code name of military operation carried by government to remove terrorists from Golden Temple complex?
    (a) Operation Reach
    (b) Operation Remove
    (c) Operation Rising Star
    (d) Operation Blue Star

12. Name the Gandhian leader who died while fasting for a separate state of Andhra Pradesh.
    (a) N. Siddharamaya
    (b) Jagjeevan Reddy
    (c) T.T. Krishnamchari
    (d) Potti Sriramulu

13. Who among the following was against the formation of states on the basis of language?
    (a) Jawaharlal Nehru
    (b) Sardar Vallabhbhai Patel
    (c) Both (a) and (b)
    (d) Potti Sriramulu

14. Which of the following became the symbol of development in Independent India?
    (a) Bridges   (b) Dams
    (c) Flag   (d) Both (a) and (b)

15. Dr. B.R. Ambedkar, the Father of Indian Constitution was a ....
    (a) Economist   (b) Lawyer
    (c) Both (a) and (b)(d) None of these

16. The Indian Constitution after its inception granted reservation in legislatures and job to ....
    (a) Scheduled Caste
    (b) Scheduled Tribes
    (c) Both (a) and (b)
    (d) None of these

17. Which of the following states were created from parts of Bihar?
    (a) Chhattisgarh   (b) Telangana
    (c) Jharkhand   (d) None of these

2 Marks Questions

18. Which of the following statement is true?
    1. Planning commission was established by government for economic development of India.
    2. The land reforms initiated after Independence were fully successful.
    Codes
    (a) Only 1   (b) Only 2
    (c) Both 1 and 2   (d) None of these

19. Which of the following statements is true?
    1. After Independence, the Indian economy was dependent mainly on agriculture.
    2. New industrial units were setup by the government through Five Year Planning.
    Codes
    (a) Only 1   (b) Only 2
    (c) Both 1 and 2   (d) None of these

20. Which of the given statement is true?
    1. The first Five Year Plan was focussed upon enhancing the agricultural sector.
    2. The second Five Year Plan focussed upon setting up industries for development of economy.
    Codes
    (a) Only 1   (b) Only 2
    (c) Both 1 and 2   (d) None of these

Chapter 07

Land, Soil and Water Resources

1 Mark Questions

1. Which of the following will be helpful in conserving the land resource?
   (a) Afforestation
   (b) Checks on overgrazing
   (c) Regulated use of pesticides
   (d) All of the above

2. Which of the following is not the factor of soil formation?
   (a) Climate   (b) Relief
   (c) Salinity   (d) Time

3. The right mix of minerals and .... make the soil fertile.
   (a) inorganic matter
   (b) organic matter
   (c) water
   (d) air

4. Which of the following methods is helpful in reducing surface runoff and soil erosion?
   (a) Mixed farming
   (b) Terrace farming
   (c) Use of chemical fertilizer
   (d) None of the above

5. Landslides are the common natural phenomena in......... .
   (a) hilly areas
   (b) desert areas
   (c) plain areas
   (d) coastal areas

6. Which of the following methods will be helpful in mitigating the risk affected by the landslides?
   (a) Hazard mapping
   (b) Construction of retention wall
   (c) Increase in vegetation cover
   (d) All of the above

7. Which one of the following is the natural factor leading to soil erosion and depletion?
   (a) Floods
   (b) Over grazing
   (c) Deforestation
   (d) Overuse of chemical fertilizers

8. Land is used for......... .
   (a) agriculture   (b) forestry
   (c) mining   (d) All of these

9. Which of the following techniques will help in preventing soil erosion?
   (a) Jhumming   (b) Irrigation
   (c) Afforestation   (d) All of these

10. Soil is made up of which of the following?
    (a) Organic matters
    (b) Minerals
    (c) Weathered rocks
    (d) All of the above

11. Shelter beds as a method for soil conservation is highly beneficial for which of the following areas?
    (a) Hilly areas
    (b) Plain areas
    (c) Coastal areas
    (d) None of the above

12. The largest amount of water resources are found in which of the following?
    (a) Rivers   (b) Ground water
    (c) Oceans   (d) Lakes

13. In the .... living beings are inter-related and interdependent on each other for survival.
    (a) Hydrosphere   (b) Atmosphere
    (c) Biosphere   (d) Lithosphere

14. Largest amount of fresh water is found in......... .
    (a) Glaciers   (b) Groundwater
    (c) Rivers   (d) Lakes

15. .... is the most precious natural resource required for the survival of human being.
    (a) Soil   (b) Air
    (c) Fresh water   (d) Sunlight

16. Which of the following types of soil is/are found in India?
    (a) Alluvial soil   (b) Red soil
    (c) Laterite soil   (d) All of these

17. Which one of the following areas is sparsely populated?
    (a) Plain areas   (b) Plateau areas
    (c) Desert areas   (d) Coastal areas

18. .... is the establishment of a forest in an area where there was no previous tree cover.
    (a) Deforestation   (b) Farming
    (c) Afforestation   (d) None of these

19. Weathering and Erosion due to rivers and streams will be maximum in which of the following regions?
    (a) Deserts   (b) Glaciers
    (c) Mountains   (d) Plateaus

20. Which of the following factors influence distribution of population?
    (a) Topography   (b) Climate
    (c) Both (a) and (b)   (d) None of these

21. The gradual wearing away of land surface materials, especially rocks, sediments, and soils, by the action of water, wind, or a glacier is called ....
    (a) Weathering   (b) Mulching
    (c) Erosion   (d) Accumulation

22. Landslides often take in conjunction with ....
    (a) Floods   (b) Earthquake
    (c) Volcanoes   (d) All of these

23. Which of the following factors contribute to the process of weathering?
    (a) Temperature changes
    (b) Frost actions
    (c) Human activities
    (d) All of the above

24. Which of the following types of soil profile contains humus?
    (a) Parent rock   (b) Weathered rock
    (c) Top soil   (d) Sub soil

2 Marks Questions

25. Which of the following techniques will help in conservation of water resources in the dry areas?

  1. Rain water harvesting
  2. Contour Bunding
  3. Micro irrigation
  4. Canal system

Codes
(a) 1, 2, 3   (b) 1, 3, 4
(c) 2, 3, 4   (d) All of these

26. Which of the following statement is true?

  1. Chemical weathering is most active in rain forest regions.
  2. If rainfall increases in a region, the rate of weathering also increases.

Codes
(a) Only 1
(b) Only 2
(c) Both 1 and 2
(d) None of the above

27. Which of the following statements is true?

  1. Many small organisms assist in soil formation by circulation of air water.
  2. Regions where there is dry climate forms soil at faster rate.

Codes
(a) Only 1   (b) Only 2
(c) Both 1 and 2   (d) None of these

28. Which of the following statement(s) is/are correct with respect to soil?

  1. The soil is the top-most layer of the earth's crust.
  2. The top layer of soil is rich in organic matter called humus.
  3. Different types of rocks such as granite, basalt and limestone are found in humus layer.

Codes
(a) Only 1 and 2   (b) Only 1 and 3
(c) Only 2 and 3   (d) 1,2 and 3

29. Which one of the following statements is not an argument in favour of multipurpose river projects?

(a) Multipurpose projects bring water to those areas which suffer from water scarcity.
(b) Multipurpose projects by regulating water flow helps to control floods.
(c) Multipurpose projects lead to large scale displacements and loss of livelihood.
(d) Multipurpose projects generate electricity for our industries and our homes.

Natural Vegetation and Wildlife

1 Mark Questions

1. Biosphere is the narrow zone of contact between the......... .
(a) Lithosphere   (c) Atmosphere
(b) Hydrosphere   (d) All of these

2. Which of the following factors affect the growth of vegetation in any area?
(a) Temperature   (b) Moisture
(c) Both (a) and (b) (d) None of these

3. Thorny shrubs and scrubs grow in ....
(a) abundant rainfall
(b) moderate rainfall
(c) moisture laden hilly areas
(d) dry areas of low rainfall

4. Mosses and lichens are the main vegetation of ....
(a) Equatorial region (b) Tundra region
(c) Temperate region (d) Monsoon region

5. Who among the following is considered as vital cleanser of the environment?
(a) Snake   (b) Crow
(c) Vultures   (d) Tiger

6. The deciduous trees shed their leaves in a particular season to......... .
(a) conserve the loss of moisture through transpiration
(b) conserve the loss of heat through transpiration

(c) conserve the loss of food through evaporation
(d) None of the above

7. The .... forest of Great Nicobar was destroyed after the Tsunami.
(a) Deciduous   (b) Temperate
(c) Rain   (d) Coniferous

8. The population of which of the following species has declined due to poaching?
(a) Rhinoceros   (b) Deer
(c) Black Buck   (d) All of these

9. In terms of area the extent of which of the following protected areas is largest?
(a) Wildlife Sanctuary
(b) Biosphere Reserve
(c) National Park
(d) Zoological park

10. Which type of vegetation grows in saline areas?
(a) Evergreen Forests
(b) Mangrove Forests
(c) Deciduous Forests
(d) Mountain Forests

11. Rain forests are found in which of the following regions of India?
(a) Western Ghats   (d) Eastern Ghats
(c) Jammu and Kashmir (d) Rajasthan

12. Evergreen forests shed their leaves in which of the following seasons?
    (a) Summer season (b) Winter season
    (c) Rainy season (d) None of these

13. The Full Form of CITES is ....
    (a) Convention on International Trade in Endangered species of Wild Fauna and Flora
    (b) Convention on International Trade in Endemic Species
    (c) Convention on International Trade in Invasive Alien Species
    (d) None of the above

14. The awareness programme .... is organised by the government at the regional and community level to protect the flora and fauna of the country.
    (a) Van Mahotsav
    (b) Vandhan
    (c) Vanjagriti
    (d) None of the above

15. Which of the following protected areas demonstrate the relationship between conservation and development?
    (a) National Park (b) Gene Bank
    (c) Biosphere Reserve
    (d) Wildlife Sanctuary

16. The highest degree of protection to the flora and fauna is provided in which of the following protected areas?
    (a) National Park
    (b) Wildlife Sanctuary
    (c) Biosphere Reserve
    (d) Bird Sanctuary

17. The Kaziranga National Park is located in which of the following states of India?
    (a) Assam (b) Madhya Pradesh
    (c) Maharashtra (d) Rajasthan

18. Gir National Park is situated in ....
    (a) Madhya Pradesh (b) Assam
    (c) Chhattisgarh (d) Gujarat

2 Marks Questions

19. Consider the following factors.
    1. Deforestation
    2. Soil erosion
    3. Forest fires
    4. Construction activities

    Which of the above is/are responsible for degradation of natural resources?
    (a) 1, 2 and 3 (b) 1, 3 and 4
    (c) 2, 3 and 4 (d) All of these

20. Which of the following pair is matched correctly?

List I (Animal)	List II (Protected Area)
1. Rhinoceroses	— Kaziranga National Park
2. Asiatic Lion	— Gir National Park
3. Cheetah	— Panna Tiger Reserve

Codes
(a) Only 1, 3 (b) Only 2, 3
(c) Only 1 and 2 (d) None of these

21. Match the following.

Forests	Trees
A. Evergreen	1. Mahogany
B. Deciduous	2. Oak
C. Coniferous	3. Teak
D. Temperate	4. Pine

Codes

	A	B	C	D		A	B	C	D
(a)	1	3	4	2	(b)	3	4	1	2
(c)	2	1	4	3	(d)	4	1	3	2

Chapter 09

Minerals and Power Resources

1 Mark Questions

1. Which among the following is a non-metallic mineral?
   (a) Iron   (b) Manganese
   (c) Bauxite   (d) Mica

2. Rocks from which minerals are mined are known as ....
   (a) Metal   (b) Non metal
   (c) Ore   (d) Metalloids

3. Drilling as a method of extraction of minerals is primarily used for ....
   (a) Petroleum   (b) Coal
   (c) Iron-ore   (d) Bauxite

4. Which of the following methods is/are utilised for extraction of minerals?
   (a) Mining   (b) Quarrying
   (c) Drilling   (d) All of these

5. The metallic minerals are generally found in which of the following rock system?
   (a) Sedimentary   (b) Igneous
   (c) Metamorphic   (d) Both (b) and (c)

6. Which of the following mineral does not have an ore?
   (a) Iron   (b) Copper
   (c) Gold   (d) Uranium

7. The rock containing copper looks .... in colour.
   (a) pink   (b) blue
   (c) black   (d) white

8. Which of the following continents is the world's largest producer of diamonds, gold and platinum?
   (a) Asia   (b) Australia
   (c) Africa   (d) Europe

9. The first country in the world to develop hydroelectricity was ....
   (a) Norway   (b) Scotland
   (c) Germany   (d) Sweden

10. Which of the following is non-conventional source of energy?
    (a) Coal
    (b) Wind Energy
    (c) Petroleum
    (d) Natural Gas

11. Nuclear energy is produced by using which of the following minerals?
    (a) Uranium
    (b) Thorium
    (c) Both (a) and (b)
    (d) Coal

12. Which one of the following minerals is formed by decomposition of rocks, leaving a residual mass of weathered material?
    (a) Coal   (b) Bauxite
    (c) Gold   (d) Zinc

13. Which among the following mineral is a metallic mineral?
    (a) Mica   (b) Manganese
    (c) Granite   (d) Sandstone

14. The leading producer of Mica in India is ....
    (a) Jharkhand   (b) Rajasthan
    (c) Chhattisgarh   (d) Andhra Pradesh

15. The Sambhar lake in Rajasthan is famous for extraction of ....
    (a) Natural gas   (b) Oil
    (c) Salt   (d) Zinc

16. Which one of the following mineral is used in computer industry?
    (a) Silicon   (b) Copper
    (c) Aluminium   (d) Radium

17. .... is the ore of Aluminium.
    (a) Monazite   (b) Chalcocite
    (c) Hematite   (d) Bauxite

18. Electricity generated from the coal is called ....
    (a) Geothermal energy
    (b) Thermal energy
    (c) Tidal energy
    (d) Solar energy

19. Which of the following is also referred as 'Buried Sunshine'?
    (a) Limestone   (b) Coal
    (c) Fossil fuel   (d) None of these

2 Marks Questions

20. Which of the following is not correct?
    (a) Petroleum and its products are called Black Gold as they are very valuable.
    (b) The leading producer of petroleum in India is Mumbai High Refinery.
    (c) Natural gas is found with petroleum deposits and is released when crude oil is brought to the surface.
    (d) Petroleum is drilled from oil fields located in peninsular areas only.

21. Which of the given pair is matched correctly?
    1. Bauxite-Metallic Mineral
    2. Gypsum-Non Metallic Mineral
    3. Cobalt-Ferrous Mineral
    Codes
    (a) Only 1 and 2   (b) Only 2 and 3
    (c) Only 1 and 3   (d) All of these

22. Which of the following pairs is not correctly matched?

	Minerals	Associated Industries
(a)	Copper	Pipe
(b)	Bauxite	Automobiles
(c)	Mica	Electronic
(d)	Gold	Construction

Agriculture

1 Mark Questions

1. Commercial rearing of silk worms is known as ....
   (a) Viticulture   (b) Sericulture
   (c) Agriculture   (d) Horticulture

2. Shifting cultivation is also known as .... in Malaysia.
   (a) Roca   (b) Jhum
   (c) Ladang   (d) Milpa

3. Which of the following elements is used in organic farming?
   (a) Chemical fertilizers
   (b) Insecticides
   (c) Natural pesticides
   (d) None of the above

4. In India, Nomadic herding is practised mainly in ....
   (a) Jammu and Kashmir
   (b) Bihar
   (c) Uttar Pradesh
   (d) Madhya Pradesh

5. The type of farming in which land is used for growing food and fodder crops and rearing livestock is called ....
   (a) Nomadic Herding
   (b) Mixed Farming
   (c) Subsistence Farming
   (d) Shifting Cultivation

6. The temperate grassland of Northern America is famous for ....
   (a) Plantation farming
   (b) Mixed farming
   (c) Commercial grain farming
   (d) Nomadic herding

7. Which of the following crops was also known as Golden fibre?
   (a) Jute   (b) Silk
   (c) Cotton   (d) Wool

8. The leading producer of rice in the world is ....
   (a) India   (b) China
   (c) Malaysia   (d) Vietnam

9. Which of the following crops is known as coarse grains?
   (a) Wheat   (b) Maize
   (c) Coffee   (d) Millets

10. Which of the following soils is most suitable for cultivation of Cotton?
    (a) Sandy soil   (b) Black soil
    (c) Red soil   (d) Arid soil

11. India and Bangladesh are leading producer of ....
    (a) Rubber   (b) Jute
    (c) Coffee   (d) Sugar

12. In which type of farming, machines are utilised on the large scale?
(a) Subsistence farming
(b) Shifting cultivation
(c) Commercial farming
(d) Mixed farming

13. .... in Africa is leading producer of Millets.
(a) Kenya   (b) Congo
(c) Nigeria   (d) Uganda

14. Which of the following animals is/are reared in Nomadic herding?
(a) Camel   (b) Sheep
(c) Yak   (d) All of these

15. Which of the following is a plantation crop?
(a) Sugarcane
(b) Rice
(c) Wheat
(d) Millets

2 Marks Questions

16. Which of the following statements is not correct?
(a) Jute grows well on alluvial soil and requires high temperature, heavy rainfall and humid climate.
(b) The cultivation of rice requires high temperature, high humidity and rainfall.
(c) Shifting cultivation is done in areas of heavy rainfall and quick regeneration of vegetation.
(d) Commercial farming is practiced in the semi-arid and arid regions of the world.

17. Which among the following statement is correct?
1. Mixed cropping involves planting two or more crops in the same field.
2. Mixed farming involves planting of crops and raising of animals.
Codes
(a) Only 1   (b) Only 2
(c) Both 1 and 2   (d) None of these

18. Which of the following pair is not correctly matched?

	Types of Agriculture	Associated Crops
(a)	Pisciculture	Fish
(b)	Viticulture	Cotton
(c)	Horticulture	Vegetables and fruits
(d)	Floriculture	Flowers

19. Match the following.

Crops	Largest Producer
A. Millets	1. India
B. Wheat	2. China
C. Coffee	3. Brazil
D. Natural Rubber	4. Thailand

Codes

	A	B	C	D		A	B	C	D
(a)	1	2	3	4	(b)	2	3	4	1
(c)	2	4	1	3	(d)	4	1	3	2

Industries

1 Mark Questions

1. Which one of the following industries is agro-based?
   - (a) Leather
   - (b) Paper
   - (c) Steel
   - (d) Coal

2. Which of the following is a type of Small Scale Industries?
   - (a) Pottery
   - (b) Iron and Steel Industries
   - (c) Paper Industries
   - (d) IT Industries

3. Major industrial regions of the world are located in the ....
   - (a) Temperate areas
   - (b) Near sea port
   - (c) Near Coal-fields
   - (d) All of these

4. Emerging industries are also known as ....
   - (a) Foot Loose Industries
   - (b) Sunrise Industries
   - (c) Cooperative Industries
   - (d) None of the above

5. Bhopal Gas leak disaster occurred due to the emission of ....
   - (a) Carbon Monoxide
   - (b) Ammonia Dioxides
   - (c) Methyl Isocyanate
   - (d) Chlorofluorocarbon

6. Which of the following industries is also known as Sunrise Industry?
   - (a) Hospitality
   - (b) Automobile
   - (c) Pharmaceuticals
   - (d) Sugar

7. In which of the following places the Iron and Steel Industry is located in India?
   - (a) Jamshedpur
   - (b) Amritsar
   - (c) Bombay High
   - (d) Khetri

8. Tata Iron and Steel Company Limited (TISCO) was started in ....
   - (a) 1905
   - (b) 1906
   - (c) 1907
   - (d) 1909

9. In India, the first successful mechanised textile mill was established in ....
   - (a) Kolkata
   - (b) Madras
   - (c) Mumbai
   - (d) Ahmedabad

10. The 'Great Lakes' industrial region is located in ....
    - (a) North America
    - (b) South America
    - (c) Asia
    - (d) Africa

11. .... is an important steel city of United States of America.
    - (a) Seattle
    - (b) Donbass
    - (c) Pittsburgh
    - (d) Santiago

12. Osaka is the major Industrial region of
……… .
(a) Japan
(b) China
(c) South Korea
(d) Russia

13. Which of the following is a secondary activity?
(a) Coal mining industry
(b) Tourism industry
(c) Fishing
(d) Agriculture

2 Marks Questions

14. Consider the following statements regarding Ahmedabad industrial region.

1. It is located in Gujarat on the banks of Narmada river.
2. After Mumbai, it is the second largest textile manufacturing city of India.

Which of the statements given above is/are correct?
(a) Only 1   (b) Only 2
(c) Both 1 and 2   (d) None of these

15. Which of the following statement is true?

1. Iron and steel is known as a basic industry.
2. Cotton textile industry is an agro-based industry.
3. Hi-Tech industries are the most advanced industry.

Codes
(a) Only 1 and 2
(b) Only 1 and 3
(c) Only 2 and 3
(d) All of the above

16. Which of the following pairs (Industries and their examples) is not correctly matched?

(a) Mineral based   – Coal Industry
(b) Sunshine Industries   – Textile Industry
(c) Forest based   – Paper
(d) Co-operative Industries   – Milk Federation

17. Match the following.

Industries/Industrial Regions	Cities
A. First Steel Industry in India	1. Ahmedabad
B. Manchester of India	2. Bengaluru
C. Cotton Capital of India	3. Jamshedpur
D. Silicon Plateau	4. Mumbai

Codes

	A	B	C	D		A	B	C	D
(a)	1	2	3	4	(b)	3	1	4	2
(c)	2	4	1	3	(d)	4	1	3	2

Chapter 12

Human Resource (Population)

1 Mark Questions

1. Which of the following countries has the highest population?
   (a) China   (b) India
   (c) Japan   (d) Russia

2. The population pyramid gives information about the ....
   (a) age
   (b) sex
   (c) Both (a) and (b)
   (d) None of the above

3. The distribution of population is highest in ....
   (a) plain areas   (b) hilly areas
   (c) desert areas   (d) rural areas

4. The difference between the birth rate and the .... of a country is called the natural growth rate.
   (a) emigration   (b) immigration
   (c) death rate   (d) None of these

5. The maximum number of countries having highest population growth is in ....
   (a) Asia   (b) Africa
   (c) Europe   (d) North America

6. In population pyramid the number of children is shown at .... and reflects the level of births.
   (a) top   (b) bottom
   (c) middle   (d) None of these

7. The population change is/are caused by ....
   (a) births
   (b) deaths
   (c) migration
   (d) All of the above

8. The population growth in which of the following countries is slowing because of both low death and low birth rate?
   (a) United Kingdom
   (b) Nigeria
   (c) Bangladesh
   (d) Kenya

9. The Human resource of any country can be enriched by ....
   (a) education
   (b) health
   (c) skilling infrastructure
   (d) All of the above

2 Marks Questions

10. Consider the following statements.

1. The difference between the birth rate and the death rate of a country is called the natural growth rate.

2. The population increase in the world is mainly due to rapid increase in natural growth rate.

Which of the statement(s) given above is/are correct?

(a) Only 1   (b) Only 2
(c) Both 1 and 2   (d) None of these

11. Which of the following statement is true?

1. A good health and education infrastructure leads to good quality of human resource

2. Developed countries are characterised by higher oldage population.

Codes
(a) Only 1   (b) Only 2
(c) Both 1 and 2   (d) None of these

12. Which of the following pairs is not correctly matched?

(a)	Birth rate	Number of live births per 1, 0000 people
(b)	Immigration	When a person enters a new country
(c)	Emigration	When a person leaves a country
(d)	Migration	Movement of people in and out of an area

13. Which of the following statement is true?

1. The continent of Asia has world's largest population.

2. Largest migrations occur from developing countries to developed countries.

Codes
(a) Only 1
(b) Only 2
(c) Both 1 and 2
(d) None of the above

Ecology and Environment

1 Mark Questions

1. Which one of the following is an example of aquatic ecosystem?
   (a) Ponds
   (b) Plateau
   (c) Desert
   (d) Mountain

2. Which one of the following represents consumers in aquatic ecosystem?
   (a) Zooplankton
   (b) Phytoplankton
   (c) Flagellates
   (d) Fungi

3. If all the plants and trees vanish from the Earth, the gas which will decrease is……… .
   (a) Carbon Dioxide
   (b) Nitrogen
   (c) Water Vapour
   (d) Oxygen

4. In the marine environment, the main primary producers are……… .
   (a) Phytoplanktons
   (b) Sea Weeds
   (c) Marie Angiosperm
   (d) Aquatic Bryophytes

5. Which of the following organism will be at the lowest level of a food chain?
   (a) Tiger
   (b) Eagle
   (c) Shrubs
   (d) Fish

6. .... is the only source of energy for all ecosystem of the world.
   (a) Wind
   (b) Sun
   (c) Soil
   (d) Water

7. Which of the following is not a biotic component of an ecosystem?
   (a) Air
   (b) Plant
   (c) Bacteria
   (d) Animals

8. Which one of the following is an artificial ecosystem?
   (a) Ponds
   (b) Fields
   (c) Forests
   (d) None of these

9. Which one of the following is the largest ecosystem of the world?
   (a) Oceans
   (b) Grassland
   (c) Forests
   (d) Mountain

10. Biomass pyramid is reversed in which type of ecosystem?
    (a) Forest
    (b) River
    (c) Desert
    (d) Grassland

11. Environment is a composite state of…… .
    (a) Biotic factors
    (b) Physiographic factors
    (c) Abiotic factors
    (d) All of the above

12. The cycling of element in an ecosystem is called………. .
(a) Chemical cycle
(b) Biogeochemical cycle
(c) Geological cycle
(d) Geochemical cycle

13. Which of the following is a biotic component of environment?
(a) River   (b) Mountain
(c) Insects   (d) Oxygen

14. Which of the following states has the largest area under the forests?
(a) Kerala   (b) Uttar Pradesh
(c) Madhya Pradesh (d) Rajasthan

15. Which of the following is the first National Park of India?
(a) Kanha National Park
(b) Dudhwa National Park
(c) Rajaji National Park
(d) Corbett National Park

16. The Chipko Movement was launched in Garhwal Himalayas for the protection of………. .
(a) forest   (b) wildlife
(c) rivers   (d) glacier

17. Ozone layer protects biosphere from ………… .
(a) Infrared rays
(b) Ultraviolet rays
(c) X-rays
(d) Gamma rays

18. In a food chain man is a………. .
(a) producer
(b) only primary consumer
(c) only secondary consumer
(d) primary as well as secondary consumer

2 Marks Questions

19. Which of the following statement is correct?
1. Environment only contains natural components of Earth.
2. When energy is transferred from one level to another, environment is degraded.

Codes
(a) Only 1   (b) Only 2
(c) Both 1 and 2   (d) None of these

20. Which of the following statement is correct?
1. The highest level of Biodiversity is found in Evergreen forests of the World.
2. Environmental degradation leads to decline in level of biodiversity.

Codes
(a) Only 1   (b) Only 2
(c) Both 1 and 2   (d) None of these

21. Match the following.

Protected Area	Examples
A. National Park	1. Panna
B. Wildlife Sanctuary	2. Kaziranga
C. Biosphere Reserve	3. Periyar

Codes

	A	B	C
(a)	1	2	3
(b)	2	3	1
(c)	2	1	3
(d)	1	2	3

Indian Constitution

1 Mark Questions

1. Who among the following was the chief architect of the Indian Constitution?
(a) B.N. Rau   (b) B. R. Ambedkar
(c) Rajendra Prasad   (d) Jawaharlal Nehru

2. What is Right to Equality?
(a) Fundamental Duty
(b) Directive Principles
(c) Fundamental Right
(d) Special Provision

3. The Constituent Assembly was established in ………… .
(a) 1948   (b) 1946
(c) 1947   (d) 1950

4. Which of the following is the organ of the state?
(a) Judiciary   (b) Legislative
(c) Executive   (d) All of these

5. How many parts are there in the Constitution of India?
(a) Ten   (b) Fifteen
(c) Twenty-Five   (d) None of these

6. Which one of the following is not the tier of Government in India?
(a) Union Government
(b) Regional Government
(c) State Government
(d) Panchayati Raj

7. According to the Constitution, there are ……… organs of government.
(a) three   (b) four   (c) five   (d) two

8. How many Fundamental Duties have been provided in our Constitution?
(a) 11   (c) 8   (b) 15   (d) 9

9. Which of the following Rights allows citizens to move the court if their Fundamental Rights are violated by the State?
(a) Right to Freedom
(b) Right Against Exploitation
(c) Right to Constitutional Remedies
(d) Right to Equality

10. Which one of the following democratic rights has not been provided to Indian citizens?
(a) Right to Vote
(b) Right to Contest Election
(c) Right to Recall
(d) Right to Information

11. Who among the following was not the member of Constituent Assembly?
(a) Mahatma Gandhi
(b) Jawaharlal Nehru
(c) John Mathai
(d) Rajendra Prasad

2 Marks Questions

12. Consider the following statements.

1. Indian Constitution provides for the three tiers of Government at Union, State and Local level.

2. The states are the agents of Union Government and draw their authority and finances from them.

Which of the statements given above is/are correct?

(a) Only 1   (b) Only 2

(c) Both 1 and 2   (d) None of these

13. Which of the following statement is true?

1. The aims and objectives of Indian Constitution are mentioned at the end of the Constitution.

2. The Constitution gives equality to all people irrespective of their caste.

Codes

(a) Only 1   (b) Only 2

(c) Both 1 and 2   (d) None of these

14. Which of the following rights are Fundamental Rights mentioned in the Constitution?

1. Right to Equality

2. Right to Freedom

3. Right to Strike

4. Right to Vote

Codes

(a) Only 2, 3   (b) Only 3, 4

(c) Only 1, 2   (d) All of these

15. Which of the following statement is correct?

1. Indian Constitution was made in 5 years.

2. The Constitution was mentioned the date of adoption.

3. Indian Constitution is the largest written Constitution.

Codes

(a) Only 2, 3   (b) Only 1, 3

(c) Only 1, 2   (d) All of these

Our Parliament

1 Mark Questions

1. The election for Lok Sabha is usually held after......... .
   (a) 5 years   (b) 6 years
   (c) 4 years   (d) None of these

2. Which of the following representative house is not subject to dissolution?
   (a) Lok Sabha
   (b) Rajya Sabha
   (c) State Legislative Assembly
   (d) None of the above

3. The Parliament of India consists of ....
   (a) Lok Sabha   (b) Rajya Sabha
   (c) President   (d) All of these

4. Which House of Parliament elects members by direct elections?
   (a) Rajya Sabha   (b) Lok Sabha
   (c) Both (a) and (b) (d) Upper House

5. Who among the following is the Chairman of Lok Sabha?
   (a) Vice-President   (b) Speaker
   (c) President   (d) Prime Minister

6. Who among the following nominates the 12 members to the Rajya Sabha?
   (a) Chairman of the Rajya Sabha
   (b) Chief Justice of India
   (c) President
   (d) Prime Minister

7. The session of the Parliament begins with the......... .
   (a) Zero hour   (b) Question hour
   (c) Debate hour   (d) Motion hour

8. In Lok Sabha the Member of Parliament (MP) represents the ....
   (a) states
   (b) districts
   (c) religious community
   (d) caste community

9. The Rajya Sabha is presided by ....
   (a) Speaker   (b) President
   (c) Vice President   (d) Prime Minister

10. Which of the following body has power to make laws for entire country?
    (a) The Lok Sabha   (b) The Rajya Sabha
    (c) President   (d) The Parliament

11. The Prime Minister of India is the leader of which party?
    (a) Opposition Party (b) Ruling Party
    (c) Minority Party   (d) None of these

12. When different political parties join together with similar concerns they are known as?
    (a) Opposition Government
    (b) Ruling Party
    (c) Coalition Government
    (d) State Government

2 Marks Questions

13. Which of the following statements is not correct?

(a) The Ministries of the Union Government are located in New Delhi.

(b) The Prime Minister Office (PMO) is in the South Block building in New Delhi.

(c) For elections to the Rajya Sabha the country is divided into number of constituencies.

(d) Law making is the significant function of the Parliament.

14. Consider the following functions regarding ' Lok Sabha'.

1. It is the biggest house in the Parliament.

2. Its members are elected every five years.

Which of the statements given above is/are correct?

(a) Only 1   (b) Only 2

(c) Both 1 and 2   (d) None of these

15. Consider the following statements.

1. In a democracy the government is formed after election.

2. The basic premise of democracy is the idea of consent.

Which of the statements given above is/are correct?

(a) Only 1   (b) Only 2

(c) Both 1 and 2   (d) None of these

16. Which of the following statement is true?

1. The Rajya Sabha members represents a particular state.

2. The Rajya Sabha is known as Upper House of Parliament.

Codes

(a) Only 1   (b) Only 2

(c) Both 1 and 2   (d) None of these

17. Which of the following pairs is not correctly matched?

	List I	List II
(a)	Decision to maintain peace with neighbouring countries	State Government
(b)	Construction of State highways	State Government
(c)	Decision to induct new aircrafts	Central Government
(d)	Decision to print new currency	Central Government

Our Judiciary

1 Mark Questions

1. Which of the following best describes the judicial system that provides a mechanism for resolving disputes?
   (a) Dispute resolution
   (b) Judicial resolution
   (c) Judicial review
   (d) None of the above

2. The Indian Judiciary is……… .
   (a) Independent
   (b) Integrated
   (c) Both (a) and (b)
   (d) None of the above

3. Which was the earliest court to be setup in India?
   (a) Madras High Court
   (b) Calcutta High Court
   (c) Bombay High Court
   (d) Delhi High Court

4. The highest court of India, the Supreme Court was established on……… .
   (a) 26th January, 1948
   (b) 15th August, 1947
   (c) 26th January, 1950
   (d) 24th January, 1951

5. The full form of PIL is……… .
   (a) Public Interest Litigation
   (b) Private Interest Libility
   (c) Poor Interest Litigation
   (d) Powerful Indebted List

6. There are ……… different layers of courts in our country.
   (a) three (b) two   (c) five   (d) six

7. Which of the following is the highest court in a state?
   (a) District Court
   (b) Supreme Court
   (c) High Court
   (d) Metropolitan Court

8. The common High Court at Chandigarh is provided for………… .
   (a) Punjab
   (b) Haryana
   (c) Both (a) and (b)
   (d) Himachal Pradesh

9. Which of the following is the Subordinate Court in India?
   (a) Additional Session Court
   (b) Trial Court
   (c) District Court
   (d) All of the above

10. Which of the following branch of law deals with any harm or injury to rights of individuals?
    (a) Civil Law
    (b) Criminal Law
    (c) Human Rights
    (d) None of the above

11. Which of the following court is a common High Court for two States?
(a) Delhi Hight Court
(b) Kolkata Hight Court
(c) Patna Hight Court
(d) All of the above

12. Who among the following are the key players in the Criminal Justice System?
(a) Police
(b) Public Prosecuter
(c) Judiciary
(d) All of these

13. The Full form of FIR is ………. .
(a) First Investigation Report
(b) First Information Report
(c) First Indication Report
(d) None of the above

14. Which court is the highest court of appeal in India?
(a) Delhi Hight Court
(b) Metropolitan Magistrate Court
(c) Supreme Court
(d) District Court

2 Marks Questions

15. Consider the following statements regarding structure of judiciary in India.

1. There are four different levels of the courts in the country.
2. The Supreme Court is the highest court of the land and is presided by the Chief Justice of India.

Which of the statements given above is/are correct?
(a) Only 1
(b) Only 2
(c) Both 1 and 2
(d) None of the above

16. Which of the following pair is matched correctly?

High Court	Other Jurisdiction
A. Kolkata High Court	1. Andamand and Nicobar
B. Madras High Court	2. Puducherry
C. Bombay High Court	3. Goa

Codes
(a) Only 1 and 2
(b) Only 2 and 3
(c) Only 1 and 3
(d) All of the above

17. Match the following.

High Courts		Located at
A. Andhra Pradesh	1.	Nainital
B. Chhattisgarh	2.	Amravati
C. Kerala	3.	Ernakulum
D. Uttarakhand	4.	Bilaspur

Codes

	A	B	C	D
(a)	1	2	3	4
(b)	2	4	3	1
(c)	3	4	1	2
(d)	4	1	3	2

18. Which of the following statement is true?

1. The powers of Supreme Court are defined in the Indian Constitution.
2. The Parliament of India has the authority to appoint Judges of Supreme Court.

Codes
(a) Only 1
(b) Only 2
(c) Both 1 and 2
(d) None of the above

Science and Technology

1 Mark Questions

1. The crops which are grown in the rainy season are called as………. .
   - (a) Kharif crops
   - (b) Rabi crops
   - (c) Zayad crops
   - (d) None of these

2. Rhizobium bacteria are present in the nodules of the roots of ………. .
   - (a) Fodder crops
   - (b) Millets
   - (c) Leguminous plant
   - (d) Fruits and vegetables

3. Which of the following diseases is/are caused by the virus?
   - (a) Polio
   - (b) Chickenpox
   - (c) Influenza
   - (d) All of these

4. Which of the following bacterias helps in the formation of curd?
   - (a) Salmonella Typhi
   - (b) Lactobacillus
   - (c) Escherichia Coli
   - (d) Bacillus Coagulans

5. The process by which a solid changes to gas without becoming a liquid is called …………. .
   - (a) Vapourisation
   - (b) Sublimation
   - (c) Boiling
   - (d) Absorption

6. Female Anopheles mosquito is the carrier of parasite of ………. .
   - (a) Dengue
   - (b) Malaria
   - (c) Small Pox
   - (d) Chicken Pox

7. Which one of the following is an example of thermosetting plastic?
   - (a) Rayon
   - (b) Polythene
   - (c) Bakelite
   - (d) Polyester

8. …………. are those species of plants and animals which are found exclusively in a particular area.
   - (a) Invasive species
   - (b) Endemic species
   - (c) Endangered species
   - (d) Protected species

9. Cell was discovered by………. .
   - (a) Robert Hook
   - (b) Watson and Creek
   - (c) Hargobind Khurrana
   - (d) James Watt

10. Which of the following is known as the Power House of the cell?
    - (a) Cell Membrane
    - (b) Cytoplasm
    - (c) Nucleus
    - (d) Mithocondria

11. Which of the following hormones is responsible for development of secondary sexual characters in girls?
    (a) Testosterone   (b) Estrogen
    (c) Relaxin   (d) Serotonin

12. All human beings have .... pairs of chromosomes in the nuclei of their cells.
    (a) 22   (b) 23
    (c) 24   (d) 21

13. The image is formed on which part of the eye?
    (a) Iris   (b) Cons
    (c) Pupil   (d) Retina

14. Visually impaired persons can read and write using the ....
    (a) Braille system   (b) Louis system
    (c) Kepler system   (d) Newton system

15. Legumes are highly nutritious because they are rich in......... .
    (a) fat   (b) protein
    (c) oil   (d) starch

16. The malfunctioning of thyroid gland is due to the deficiency of......... .
    (a) Vitamin A   (b) Calcium
    (c) Iodine   (d) Iron

17. The calorific value of which of the following fuel is highest?
    (a) Biogas   (b) CNG
    (c) Hydrogen   (d) Diesel

18. Friction can be increased by making a surface......... .
    (a) soft   (b) rough
    (c) polished   (d) None of these

19. Light-year is a unit of ....
    (a) time   (b) speed
    (c) distance   (d) intensity of light

20. The incomplete burning of petrol and diesel produces ....
    (a) Nitric Oxide
    (b) Nitrogen Dioxide
    (c) Carbon Dioxide
    (d) Carbon Monoxide

21. The second person to land on moon after Neil Armstrong was......... .
    (a) Yuri Gagarin   (b) Leonov
    (c) Michael Collins   (d) Edwin Aldrin

22. The speed of the sound is highest in ....
    (a) water   (b) air
    (c) steel   (d) vacuum

23. Tungsten is metal used in the filament of incandescent bulbs. What is the chemical symbol of Tungsten?
    (a) W   (b) Au
    (c) Ag   (d) Cu

24. Which of these elements is needed to make nuclear energy and nuclear weapons?
    (a) Sodium Chloride
    (b) Uranium
    (c) Nitrogen
    (d) Carbon Dioxide

25. The first satellite launched by India was......... .
    (a) Aryabhata   (b) Bhaskara 1
    (c) Bhaskara 2   (d) Rohini

2 Marks Questions

26. Which of the following pairs is not correctly matched?

Human/Plant Disease	Causative Organism
(a) Malaria	Protozoa
(b) Hepatitis A	Fungi
(c) Citrus canker	Bacteria
(d) Yellow vein mosaic of okra	Virus

27. Which of the following statement is correct?

1. Electroplating of metal can be done to prevent rusting.
2. Electroplating increases the strength of metal.

Codes
(a) Only 1
(b) Only 2
(c) Both 1 and 2
(d) None of the above

28. Match the following.

List I	List II
A. Polyster	1. Prepared by using wood pulp
B. Teflon	2. Used for making parachutes and stockings
C. Rayon	3. Used to make non-stick cookwares
D. Nylon	4. Fabrics do not wrinkle easily

Codes

	A	B	C	D		A	B	C	D
(a)	1	4	3	2	(b)	4	3	1	2
(c)	3	2	4	1	(d)	4	1	3	2

29. Which of the following is a synthetic fibre?

1. Acrylic   2. Jute
3. Rayon   4. Nylon

Codes
(a) 1, 2, 3   (b) 2, 3, 4
(c) 1, 3, 4   (d) All of these

Chapter 18

Computers

1 Mark Questions

1. Which of the following is known as brain of the computer?
   (a) Monitor
   (b) Central Processing Unit
   (c) Keyboard
   (d) Hard disk

2. Identify the first generation computer from the given options.
   (a) PARAM
   (b) ENIAC
   (c) SIERRA
   (d) FUGAKU

3. Ctrl, Shift and Alt are called .... keys.
   (a) modifers
   (b) alphanumeric
   (c) function
   (d) adjustment

4. Which key is used in combination with another key to perform a specific task?
   (a) Function
   (b) Spacebar
   (c) Arrow
   (d) Control

5. A very high speed memory is placed between the CPU and the primary memory known as ....
   (a) Cache
   (b) Read Only Memory (ROM)
   (c) Secondary memory
   (d) Random Access Memory (RAM)

6. Which type of computer could be found in a digital watch?
   (a) Analog computer
   (b) Digital computer
   (c) Mainframe computer
   (d) Embedded computer

7. Which among the following is secondary storage device?
   (a) Hard Disk
   (b) RAM
   (c) Diode
   (d) Semi Conductor

8. 1 Mega Byte is equal to.......... .
   (a) 1024 Bytes
   (b) 1024 Kilo Bytes
   (c) 1024 Giga Bits
   (d) 1024 Bits

9. An electronic path, which sends signals from one part of computer to another is called ....
   (a) Logic gate
   (b) Modem
   (c) Bus
   (d) Serial Port

10. Systemically designed step-by-step guidelines generally written in simple English language are called ....
    (a) Algorithm
    (b) Compiler
    (c) Interpreter
    (d) None of these

11. In a typical e-mail address Rohit@ gmail.com, Rohit is a ....
    (a) Host name
    (b) Domain name
    (c) User name
    (d) Sign

12. The full form of ISP is ....
(a) Internet Service Provider
(b) Integrated Service Provider
(c) Information Service Provider
(d) International Service Provider

13. A document or image stored on the hard disk or pen drive is referred to as a ....
(a) Hard copy   (b) Soft copy
(c) Digital copy   (d) None of these

14. Which one of the following is not an example of operating system?
(a) Windows   (b) Android
(c) Google Chrome   (d) Fedora

15. Which of the following is a programming language in computers?
(a) Java
(b) Swift
(c) C++
(d) All of the above

2 Marks Questions

16. Which of the following statements is true?
1. Local Area Network can be used to connect computer systems of one city to another.
2. Wide Area Networks can be used to connect computer systems of two countries.
3. Personal Area Networks are smallest networks.

Codes
(a) Only 1, 2   (b) Only 2, 3
(c) Only 1, 3   (d) All of these

17. Consider the following statements.
1. A computer system uses binary numbers to store and process data.
2. Secondary memory is of two types Random Access Memory (RAM) and Read Only Memory (ROM).

Which of the statement(s) given above is/are correct?
(a) Only 1   (b) Only 2
(c) Both 1 and 2   (d) None of these

18. Consider the following statements.
1. An antivirus is utility software which detects and removes computer viruses.
2. Boot sector virus can infect softwares on a computer.

Which of the statement(s) given above is/are correct?
(a) Only 1   (b) Only 2
(c) Both 1 and 2   (d) All of these

19. Which of the following pair is not correctly matched?

	Functions	Shortcut Keys
(a)	Opening a new document	Ctrl + N
(b)	Saving a document	Ctrl + S
(c)	Opening a document	Ctrl + O
(d)	Pasting the selected items	Ctrl + A

20. Match the following.

	Generation of Computers		Characterised by
A.	First Generation	1.	Microprocessor
B.	Second Generation	2.	Vaccum Tube
C.	Third Generation	3.	Integrated Chips
D.	Fourth Generation	4.	Transistor

Codes

	A	B	C	D		A	B	C	D
(a)	1	3	2	4	(b)	2	4	3	1
(c)	3	2	4	1	(d)	4	1	3	2

Chapter 19

General Knowledge

1 Mark Questions

1. The first person to land on Moon was ....
   (a) Neil Armstrong (b) Yuri Gagarin
   (c) Edwin Aldrin   (d) Michael Collins

2. The first female Vice President of United States of America is ....
   (a) Tulsi Gabbarad   (b) Meena Harris
   (c) Kamla Harris   (d) Ivanca Trump

3. The first Indian to win Nobel Prize was ....
   (a) C.V. Raman
   (b) Rabindranath Tagore
   (c) Mother Teresa
   (d) Hargovind Khurana

4. Who was the first man to climb Mt. Everest?
   (a) Tenzing Norgay (b) Bachendri Pal
   (c) Rechard Wass   (d) None of these

5. The first country to introduce paper currency was ....
   (a) India   (b) China
   (c) Russia   (d) Japan

6. Which among the following is the largest tiger reserve in India?
   (a) Kanha National park
   (b) Bhandavgarh National park
   (c) Nagarajuna Srisailam
   (d) Jim Corbett National Park

7. Name the Indian state with the largest coastline?
   (a) Andhra Pradesh
   (b) Gujarat
   (c) Maharashtra
   (d) Kerala

8. The fastest Indian train is ....
   (a) Gatimaan Express
   (b) Kalka Shatabadi
   (c) Vande Bharat Express
   (d) Duronto Express

9. Which among the following state is the biggest producer of the rice in India?
   (a) West Bengal   (b) Uttar Pradesh
   (c) Punjab   (d) Andhra Pradesh

10. The Indian state with the largest population of Indian Rhinoceros is ....
    (a) West Bengal
    (b) Assam
    (c) Arunachal Pradesh
    (d) Madhya Pradesh

11. Who among the following is the 'Father of Green Revolution' in India?
    (a) Verghees Kurien
    (b) Ashok Gulati
    (c) M. Swaminathan
    (d) N. Chandrashekran

12. Who among the following is the 'Father of Cryogenic Engine' in India?
    (a) K. Sivan
    (b) Homi Bhabha
    (c) A.S. Kiran Kumar
    (d) Nambi Narayan

13. Who among the following is referred as 'Father of Civil Aviation' in India?
    (a) J.R.D. Tata
    (b) Satish Dhawan
    (c) N. Chandrashekran
    (d) D. Rustom Ji

14. Who among the following is popularly known as Mother of Indian Revolution?
    (a) Kasturba Gandhi (b) Bhikaji Kama
    (c) Aruna Asaf Ali   (d) Annie Besant

15. Shakti sthal is the crematorium of which of the following?
    (a) Mahatma Gandhi
    (b) Rajiv Gandhi
    (c) Indira Gandhi
    (d) Lal Bahadur Shastri

16. Alfred Nobel is credited with which of the following inventions?
    (a) Diesel Engive   (b) Dynamite
    (c) Jet Engine   (d) Rubber

17. 'Calicut' was the old name of which city?
    (a) Mysore   (b) Kochi
    (c) Kozhikode   (d) Ernakulam

18. What was the old name of 'Kanyakumari'?
    (a) Cape Comorin   (b) Coromandel
    (c) Palghat   (d) Kovalam

2 Marks Questions

19. Which of the following pairs is not correctly matched?

	First in India	Personalities
(a)	First Women State Governor in India	Sarojini Naidu
(b)	First Women President of Indian National Congress	Annie Besant
(c)	First Women Speaker of Lok Sabha	Meira Kumar
(d)	First Women Chief Election Commissioner	Gita Gopinath

20. Consider the following statements regarding Indian states.
    1. Rajasthan is the largest state in India.
    2. Amongst states, Bihar has the highest population in India.
    3. Sikkim is the least populated state in India.

    Which of the statement(s) given above is/are correct?
    (a) Both 1 and 2
    (b) Both 1 and 3
    (c) Both 2 and 3
    (d) All of the above

21. Kochi is located in the state of Kerala. Known as the Queen of the Arabian sea, Kochi was an important port on the spice trade route. What was it called before being reanamed in 1996?
    (a) Koti   (b) Coorg
    (c) Cochin   (d) Cotachi

Chapter 20

Defence

1 Mark Questions

1. The Supreme Commander of Indian Armed forces is......... .
(a) President
(b) Prime Minister
(c) Defence Minister
(d) Chief of Defence Staff

2. Who is known as the 'Father of Indian Missile Technology'?
(a) Satish Dhawan
(b) Dr. APJ Abdul Kalam
(c) Dr. Homi Bhabha
(d) Dr. Chidambram

3. Supersonic Cruise Missile Brahmos is joint venture of which of the following?
(a) India and Japan
(b) India and USA
(c) India and France
(d) India and Russia

4. India's anti-tank missile is......... .
(a) Nag
(b) Agni
(c) Prithvi
(d) Akash

5. The first indigenously developed anti-radiation missile of India is......... .
(a) Tejashvi
(b) Marut
(c) Garuda
(d) Rudram

6. Which of the following was the first sub marine developed by India?
(a) INS Kaveri
(b) INS Kalvari
(c) INS Arjun
(d) None of these

7. What is India's first indigenous aircraft carrier called?
(a) Vikrant
(b) Virat
(c) Vaibha
(d) Varaha

8. The first chief of the Army staff of India was ....
(a) Rajendrasinhji Jadeja
(b) K.M. Cariappa
(c) Dalbir Singh Suhag
(d) Bipin Rawat

9. Which of the following agency was established immediately aftermath of Mumbai attack?
(a) National Security Force
(b) Research and Analysis Wing
(c) National Investigation Agency
(d) Intelligence Bureau

10. The military exercise 'Indra' is conducted between India and ....
(a) USA
(b) Israel
(c) Japan
(d) Russia

11. The first Chief of Defence Staff of India is ....
(a) Bipin Rawat
(b) M. M. Narvane
(c) Vinod Singh
(d) None of these

12. Which of the following paramilitary forces was the first force to raise an all-woman battalion in India?
(a) ITBP
(b) BSF
(c) CRPF
(d) CISF

2 Marks Questions

13. Which of the following pair is not matched correctly?

Defence Equipment	Functions
A. Bhishma	Battle Tank
B. Barak	Fighter Jet
C. Agni	Missile
D. Chetak	Helicopter

14. Which of the following pairs is not correctly matched?

Defence Position Name of the Person

(a) First Chief of Defence Staff–General Sam Maneksaw

(b) First Defence Minister-Baldev Singh

(c) First Commander-in-Chief-Field Marshal K.M. Cariyappa of Indian Army

(d) First Chief of Army Staff-Rajendra Sinhji Jadeja

15. Which of the following pair is/are correct?

1. CRPF-Central Regional Police Force

2. CISF-Central Industrial Security Force

3. ITBP–Indo Tibetan Border Police

Codes

(a) Only 1 and 2

(b) Only 1 and 3

(c) Only 2 and 3

(d) All of the above

16. Which of the following pair is matched correctly?

List I (Defence Equipment)	List II (Type)
1. Brahmos	Supersonic Missile
2. Cheetah	Helicopter
3. Mirage	Fighter Jet
4. Arjun	Main Battle Tank

Codes

(a) Only 1 and 2

(b) Only 2 and 3

(c) Only 1, 2 and 4

(d) All of the above

International Organisation

1 Mark Questions

1. Headquarters of United Nations Organisation is located at which place?
   (a) Geneva   (b) New York
   (c) Rome   (d) Washington

2. The headquarters of World Health Organisation is in ....
   (a) Paris   (b) Singapore
   (c) Geneva   (d) Vienna

3. The headquarters of World Trade Organisation (WTO) is located at
   (a) Geneva   (b) Paris
   (c) Hague   (d) Nairobi

4. The headquarters of Asian Infrastructure and Investment Bank is located in ....
   (a) Shanghai   (b) Jakarta
   (c) Beijing   (d) Bangkok

5. Which of the following International organisation gives World Heritage Status to monuments and places?
   (a) WTO   (b) UNICEF
   (c) UNESCO   (d) WHO

6. Who among the following is not member of G-7?
   (a) France   (b) Germany
   (c) Russia   (d) USA

7. Which one of the following countries is not the member of the BRICS, intergovernmental organisation?
   (a) Brazil   (b) Russia
   (c) South Korea   (d) India

8. Which of the following UN organ promotes the rights and well being of every child?
   (a) UNICEF
   (b) WHO
   (c) League of Nation
   (d) ILO

9. Which of the following institutions is not a part of the World Bank Community?
   (a) IBRD   (b) WTO
   (c) IDA   (d) IFC

10. World Bank's headquarter is located at ....
    (a) Manila
    (b) Washington DC
    (c) New York
    (d) Geneva

11. The headquarters of International Atomic Energy Agency is located in ....
    (a) Vienna   (b) London
    (c) Geneva   (d) Washington

12. First Indian to make a speech in Hindi before the UN General Assembly is ………… .
    - (a) Moraji Desai
    - (b) A.B. Vajpayee
    - (c) Lal Bahadur Shastri
    - (d) Lal Krishna Advani

13. Which among the following is the oldest International organisation?
    - (a) WHO-World Health Organisation
    - (b) WTO–World Trade Organisation
    - (c) International Telegraph Union
    - (d) World Bank

2 Marks Questions

14. Which one of the following statement is not correct?
    - (a) United Nations Day is celebrated on 24th October every year.
    - (b) There are six principle organisation of the United Nations.
    - (c) General Assembly is the most powerful organ of United Nations.
    - (d) United Nations was setup after World War II.

15. Consider the following statements regarding European Union.
    1. It consists of 27 member states lying predominately in the Europe.
    2. It provides for free movement, European citizenship and common currency for its member states.

    Which of the statement(s) given above is/are correct?
    - (a) Only 1
    - (b) Only 2
    - (c) Both (1) and (2)
    - (d) None of the above

16. Which of the following pairs is matched correctly?
    - (a) ASEAN–Association of South East Asian Nations
    - (b) SAARC–South American Association for Regional Cooperation
    - (c) APEC–Asia Pacific Economic Cooperation
    - (d) Only (a) and (c)

17. Match the following pair.

	List I (Organisation)	List II (Purpose)
A.	INTERPOL	1. Nuclear Energy
B.	IAEA	2. Social and Economic Development
C.	UNDP	3. Police Organisation

Codes

	A	B	C			A	B	C
(a)	3	2	1		(b)	1	2	3
(c)	3	1	2		(d)	2	3	1

Chapter 22

Sports

1 Mark Questions

1. The national game of which of the following country is same as of India?
   - (a) Bangladesh
   - (b) Sri Lanka
   - (c) Pakistan
   - (d) Nepal

2. The first Asian Games were held in 1951 in which country?
   - (a) India
   - (b) China
   - (c) Indonesia
   - (d) South Korea

3. The first modern Olympic Games were started in the Athens in ....
   - (a) 1904
   - (b) 1896
   - (c) 1908
   - (d) 1900

4. Who was the first Indian to qualify for Olympics?
   - (a) Shiny Abraham
   - (b) P.T. Usha
   - (c) Karnam Malleshwari
   - (d) Jyotirmoyee Sikdar

5. Abhinav Bindra won Gold Medal in Men's 10 m air rifile at which of the following Olympics?
   - (a) Beijing Olympics
   - (b) London Olympics
   - (c) Rio de Janerio Olympics
   - (d) Athens Olympics

6. In which sports, PV Sindhu won the silver medal at the Rio de Janerio Olympics?
   - (a) Wrestling
   - (b) Tennis
   - (c) Boxing
   - (d) Badminton

7. India won its second 50 over Cricket World Cup in ....
   - (a) 1983
   - (b) 1992
   - (c) 2007
   - (d) 2011

8. Which among the following Grand Slam tournaments is oldest?
   - (a) Australia Open
   - (b) French Open
   - (c) Wimbledon
   - (d) US Open

9. Durand Cup is associated with which one of the following sporting events in India?
   - (a) Hockey
   - (b) Football
   - (c) Cricket
   - (d) Kabbadi

10. Mirabai Chanu is associated with which of the following sports?
    - (a) Badminton
    - (b) Weightlifting
    - (c) Wrestling
    - (d) Javelin Throw

11. Which tennis player has won India's only tennis medal at Olympic Games?
    - (a) Sania Mirza
    - (b) Leander Paes
    - (c) Mahesh Bhupati
    - (d) Rohan Bopanna

12. The world biggest cricket stadium is located in which of the following state?
    - (a) Uttar Pradesh
    - (b) Haryana
    - (c) Gujarat
    - (d) Karnataka

13. Captain Roop Singh Stadium is associated with which sport?
    (a) Hockey   (b) Cricket
    (c) Badminton   (d) Golf

14. Wellington Trophy is related to which game?
    (a) Rowing   (b) Hockey
    (c) Tennis   (c) Polo

15. With which game does Santosh Trophy is associated?
    (a) Tennis   (b) Cricket
    (c) National Football (d) Golf

16. Which of the following International Tennis Tournaments is held on grass court?
    (a) US open
    (b) French Open
    (c) Wimbledon
    (d) Australian Open

17. Boat race is a famous festival game of ....
    (a) Tamil Nadu   (b) Kerala
    (c) Goa   (d) Assam

18. What is the new name of Feroz Shah Kotla ground?
    (a) Arun Jaitley Stadium
    (b) Sheila Dikshit Stadium
    (c) Gautam Gambhir Stadium
    (d) Ajit Wadekar Stadium

19. For which of the following games/sports the term Ring is not used for ground/playing space?
    (a) Boxing   (b) Gymnastics
    (c) Ice Hockey   (d) Baseball

20. In which of the following years the Khelo India Youth Games was started in India?
    (a) 2017   (b) 2018
    (c) 2016   (d) 2019

2 Marks Questions

21. Match List I with List II.

List I (Term)		List II (Sport)	
A.	Bull's Eye	1.	Cricket
B.	Caddy	2.	Tennis
C.	Deuce	3.	Shooting
D.	Googly	4.	Golf

Codes

	A	B	C	D		A	B	C	D
(a)	1	2	3	4	(b)	4	2	3	1
(c)	2	1	3	4	(d)	3	4	2	1

22. Consider the following statements regarding Indian Premier League (IPL).

    1. It is associated with Cricket.

    2. It was first organised in 2008.

    3. It has never been organised outside India.

Which of the statement(s) given above is/are correct?
    (a) Both 1 and 2   (b) Both 1 and 3
    (c) Both 2 and 3   (d) All of these

23. Match the following.

List I (Cup/Trophies)		List II (Associated Sports)	
(a)	UEFA	1.	Football
(b)	Thomas Cup	2.	Badminton
(c)	Davis Cup	3.	Tennis
(d)	The Ashes	4.	Test Cricket

Codes

	A	B	C	D
(a)	1	2	3	4
(b)	2	3	1	4
(c)	4	1	3	2
(d)	3	4	2	1

PRACTICE SET 

1 Mark Questions

1. The fine qualities of cotton and silk produced during 17th century in India had a big market in ....
   (a) Africa (b) Europe
   (c) England (d) Indonesia

2. As an alternative to Indigo that the Indians produced, the Europeans heavily depended upon which plant to produce violet and blue dyes?
   (a) Rice (b) Woad
   (c) Vat (d) Sugarcane

3. Birsa belonged to which of the following tribes?
   (a) Oraons (b) Santhals
   (c) Mundas (d) Khonds

4. Which of the following tribes were reluctant to work for others and saw themselves as people of the forest who could only live on the produce of the forests?
   (a) Baigas (b) Bhils
   (c) Bonda (d) Banjara

5. Which Mughal ruler was proclaimed as the leader of the 1857 Revolt?
   (a) Shah Alam II (b) Alamgir
   (c) Bahadur Shah (d) Ahmed Shah

6. Who among the following was the leader of 1857 revolt in Lucknow?
   (a) Bijris Qadr (b) Laxmi Bai
   (c) Mangal Pandey (d) Bahadur Shah

7. When was Delhi recaptured by the Britishers from the rebel forces?
   (a) September 1857 (b) September 1858
   (c) August 1857 (d) August 1858

8. Who among the following is known as the Father of Bengal Renaissance?
   (a) Ishwar Chandra Vidyasagar
   (b) Raja Ram Mohan Roy
   (c) Swami Dayananda Saraswati
   (d) Veerasalingam Pantulu

9. Who was the founder of Hindustan Socialist Republic Association?
   (a) Mahatma Gandhi
   (b) Subhash Chandra Bose
   (c) Chandrasekhar Azad
   (d) Jawaharlal Nehru

10. The first session of Indian National Congress was held in ....
    (a) Delhi (b) Lucknow
    (c) Ludhiana (d) Bombay

11. Which of the following National Movement boycotted British foreign cloth and adopted India made cloth?
    (a) Quit India Movement
    (b) Swadeshi Movement
    (c) Civil Disobedience Movement
    (d) Non-Cooperation Movement

12. The Akali agitation rose in which part of India?
    (a) Punjab (b) Bengal
    (c) Hyderabad (d) Jammu

13. Who among the following argued for the policy of Non-alignment in the United Nations?
    (a) Krishna Menon
    (b) Swami Dayananda Saraswati
    (c) Subhash Chandra Bose
    (d) Muhammad Jinnah

14. Mahatma Gandhi was assassinated on ....
    (a) 28th December, 1947
    (b) 30th january, 1948
    (c) 19th February, 1949
    (d) None of these

15. Mass Movement of rock, debris or Earth down a slope is known as........ .
    (a) Volcanoes
    (b) Earthquakes
    (c) Landslides
    (d) Tsunami

16. One of the main reasons for the formation of soil is ....
    (a) surface drainage
    (b) increase in vegetation
    (c) weathering
    (d) All of the above

17. Which of the following region is associated with the Tundra vegetation?
    (a) Polar region
    (b) Tropical region
    (c) Sub-tropical region
    (d) Equatorial region

18. Which of the following minerals does not contain iron?
    (a) Chromites   (b) Gypsum
    (c) Manganese   (d) None of these

19. Kakrapar Nuclear Power Plant was setup in which of the following state?
    (a) Rajasthan   (b) Madhya Pradesh
    (c) Tamil Nadu   (d) Gujarat

20. Rearing of silk is associated with which of the following?
    (a) Sericulture   (b) Pisiculture
    (c) Viticulture   (d) Horticulture

21. Which of the following crops requires two hundred and ten frost free days?
    (a) Maize   (b) Sugarcane
    (c) Cotton   (d) Jute

22. Basket weaving is the example of which Industry?
    (a) Large scale industry
    (b) Small scale industry
    (c) Medium industry
    (d) Startup industry

23. Where was first successful mechanised textile mill established in 1854?
    (a) Bengal   (b) Pune
    (c) Mumbai   (d) Goa

24. What is the average density population of the whole world?
    (a) 382 person per sq. km
    (b) 93 person per sq. km
    (c) 51 person per sq. km
    (d) 101 person per sq. km

25. The gas predominantly responsible for Global Warming is......... .
    (a) Nitrous Oxide
    (b) Nitrogen Peroxide
    (c) Carbon Dioxide
    (d) Carbon Monoxide

26. Which of the following is not a site for in-situ conservation?
   (a) Biosphere
   (b) Zoological Park
   (c) National Park
   (d) Wildlife Sanctuary

27. What kind of roles citizens of India play in electing their representatives?
   (a) Indirect
   (b) Direct
   (c) No role
   (d) All of these

28. The Indian Constitution was finally completed in which year?
   (a) November 1946
   (b) September 1949
   (c) November 1949
   (d) August 1950

29. The Parliament of India has how many houses?
   (a) 2
   (b) 3
   (c) 4
   (d) 5

30. In which age judge of High Court gets retired?
   (a) 62 years
   (b) 65 years
   (c) 70 years
   (d) 75 years

31. WannaCry, Petya and Eternal Blue is associated with?
   (a) Cryptocurrency
   (b) Nanotechnology
   (c) Robots
   (d) Cyber attacks

32. RAM stands for......... .
   (a) Random Access Memory
   (b) Random Access Member
   (c) Random Available Memory
   (d) Required Access Memory

33. GST stands for......... .
   (a) Government Services Tariff
   (b) Goods and Services Tax
   (c) Grand School Television
   (d) Goods and Selective Tariff

34. Which is the deepest ocean of the world?
   (a) Pacific ocean
   (b) Atlantic ocean
   (c) Indian ocean
   (d) Arctic ocean

35. RUSTOM developed by DRDO is a ....
   (a) Helicopter
   (b) Drone
   (c) Anti-tank submarine
   (d) Satellite

36. The headquarters of International Court of Justice is situated at......... .
   (a) New York
   (b) Netherlands
   (c) Rome
   (d) Switzerland

37. World Health Organisation was established in which year?
   (a) 1948 (b) 1947 (c) 1990 (d) 2000

38. Jallikattu is an ancient bull taming blood sport played in which state?
   (a) Telangana
   (b) Assam
   (c) Rajasthan
   (d) Tamil Nadu

39. How many balls are present on the table while playing snooker game?
   (a) 20 (b) 21 (c) 22 (d) 23

40. 'Oxford-Astra Zeneca' is a COVID-19 vaccine developed by which country?
   (a) UK
   (b) US
   (c) India
   (d) Russia

2 Marks Questions

41. Consider the following statements.

1. The Britishers declared forests as the state property.

2. The reserved forests produced timber which the Britishers wanted.

3. In reserved forests people were allowed to move freely.

Which of the statements given above are correct?

(a) Both 1 and 3   (b) Both 2 and 3
(c) Both 1 and 2   (d) All of these

42. Consider the following statements that were introduced aftermath of 1857 revolt.

1. The British Parliament transferred the powers of East India Company to the British Crown.

2. The Indian Council was removed.

3. The Governor General of India was given the title of Secretary of State.

Which of the statements given above are correct?

(a) Both 2 and 3   (b) Both 1 and 2
(c) Both 1 and 3   (d) None of these

43. Match the following.

List I		List II
A. Raja Ram Mohan Roy	1.	Widow Remarriage
B. Ishwar Chandra Vidyasagar	2.	Against Sati Practice
C. Dayananda Saraswati	3.	Widows Home at Poona
D. Pandita Ramabai	4.	Reform Hinduism

Codes

	A	B	C	D		A	B	C	D
(a)	2	1	4	3	(b)	1	2	3	4
(c)	3	4	1	2	(d)	4	3	2	1

44. Consider the following statements about the National Movement.

1. The Moderates were opposed to the use of boycott.

2. The Congress and the Britishers signed the historic Lucknow Pact.

3. The partition of Bengal took place in 1907.

4. Gandhiji led the first Satyagraha in India as Champaran.

Which of the statements given above are correct?

(a) Both 1 and 3   (b) Both 2 and 4
(c) Both 1 and 4   (d) Both 2 and 3

45. Match the following.

List I		List II
A. Geeta Rahasya	1.	Rabindranath Tagore
B. Geetanjali	2.	Jawaharlal Nehru
C. Discovery of India	3.	Maulana Abul Kalam Azad
D. India Wins Freedom	4.	Bal Gangadhar Tilak

Codes

	A	B	C	D		A	B	C	D
(a)	1	2	3	4	(b)	4	1	2	3
(c)	2	3	4	1	(d)	4	2	1	3

46. Consider the following statements.

    1. Major forest type of the Nanda Devi Biosphere Reserve is temperate.

    2. Nilgiri Biosphere Reserve also possesses dry scrubs and swamps.

Which of the statements given above is/are correct?

(a) Only 1   (b) Only 1

(c) Both 1 and 2   (d) Neither 1 nor 2

47. Which of the following statement is correct?

    1. Coal is found in metamorphic rocks

    2. Petroleum is obtained from sedimentary rocks.

    3. In India, the highest quality coal is found in Gondwana rocks.

Codes

(a) Only 1, 2   (b) Only 1, 3

(c) Only 2, 3   (d) All of these

48. In the Parliamentary form of Government, the members of the Council of Ministers are collectively responsible to ………. .

(a) the Prime Minister

(b) the President

(c) the Lower House of the Parliament

(d) the Upper House of the Parliament

49. Which of the following states does not have a High Court?

(a) Goa

(b) Tripura

(c) Manipur

(d) Meghalaya

50. The image formed by a convex mirror is always………. .

(a) virtual and erect

(b) real and inverted

(c) same size as that of object

(d) All of the above

PRACTICE SET 02

1 Mark Questions

1. Tipu Sultan established a close relationship with which of the following and modernised his army with their help?
   (a) English
   (b) French
   (c) Portuguese
   (d) Dutch

2. Who among the following accepted the Diwani of Bengal, Bihar and Odisha from Mughal ruler in 1765?
   (a) Charles Cornwallis
   (b) Robert Clive
   (c) Alexander Reed
   (d) Lord Dalhousie

3. Who were considered as Dikus by the tribal people?
   (a) Moneylenders
   (b) Different tribes
   (c) Forest animals
   (d) None of these

4. Who among the following was/were considered as more civilised by Britishers?
   (a) Hunter-gatherers
   (b) Shifting cultivators
   (c) Santhals
   (d) Tribal chiefs

5. Where did the famous sepoy mutiny of 1857 begin from?
   (a) Delhi
   (b) Agra
   (c) Lucknow
   (d) Meerut

6. The Britishers blamed whom in a big way for the rebellion of 1857 and treated them with suspicion and hostility?
   (a) Hindus
   (b) Sikhs
   (c) Muslims
   (d) Christians

7. In which year was Widow Remarriage Act passed by Britishers?
   (a) 1855
   (b) 1856
   (c) 1859
   (d) 1863

8. Who among the following secretly learned to read and write in the flickering light of the candles at the night?
   (a) Pandita Ramabai
   (b) Mumtaz Ali
   (c) Rashundari Debi
   (d) Begum Rokeya Hossain

9. Who was the founder of Satnami Movement in Central India?
   (a) Ghasidas
   (b) Haridas Thakur Matua
   (c) Shri Narayan Guru
   (d) Jyotirao Phule

10. Who among the following was known as Periyar?
    (a) B.R. Ambedkar
    (b) E.V. Ramaswami Naicker
    (c) Sayyid Ahmad Khan
    (d) Swami Vivekananda

11. Who announced the Partition of Bengal in 1905?
    (a) Lord Curzon
    (b) Lord Dalhousie
    (c) Lord Bentinck
    (d) Lord Williams

12. Among the following options, along with untouchables who were granted reservation in seats and jobs as per the Constitution of India?
    (a) Brahmins
    (b) Anglo-Indians
    (c) Scheduled Castes
    (d) Christians

13. .... died fasting for demand for a separate state for Telugu people.
    (a) AC Rao
    (b) Potti Sriramalu
    (c) Maulana Azad
    (d) T T Krishnamachari

14. .... was the first Foreign Minister of independent India.
    (a) Jawaharlal Nehru
    (b) Vijaya Lakshmi Pandit
    (c) Krishna Iyer
    (d) Sardar Patel

15. Top soil which includes layer of organic litter, such as fallen leaves and twigs are also known as......... .
    (a) Horizon O
    (b) Horizon A
    (c) Horizon B
    (d) Horizon C

16. .... is a method where different crops are grown in alternate rows and are sown at different times to protect the soil from rain wash.
    (a) Intercropping
    (b) Terrace farming
    (c) Mulching
    (d) Crop rotation

17. What is the man-made cause for destruction of natural vegetation and wildlife?
    (a) Earthquakes
    (b) Floods
    (c) Forest Fires
    (d) Deforestation

18. How many biosphere reserves are there in India?
    (a) 10   (b) 15   (c) 18   (d) 22

19. Which of the following is the leading producer of copper in the world?
    (a) Zimbabwe
    (b) Chile
    (c) India
    (d) China

20. Which of the following is known as Black Gold?
    (a) Natural gas
    (b) Thermal energy
    (c) Petroleum
    (d) Solar energy

21. What is obtained from Quartz?
    (a) Gold
    (b) Uranium
    (c) Bauxite
    (d) Silicon

22. The land that can be used for growing crops is known as......... .
    (a) Arable land
    (b) Fallow land
    (c) Barren land
    (d) Forest land

23. Which of the following does not fit into the categories of Commercial farming?
    (a) Commercial Grain Farming
    (b) Mixed Farming
    (c) Subsistence Farming
    (d) Plantation Agriculture

24. Silicon Valley is located in......... .
    (a) Bangalore
    (b) California
    (c) Ahmedabad
    (d) Gujarat

25. Which of the following is not the common method of classifying industries?
    (a) Raw material
    (b) Size
    (c) Ownership
    (d) Quality

26. The population explosion took place in India in which year?
    (a) 1950 (b) 1959 (c) 1965 (d) 1970

27. What is Photosynthesis?
    (a) Using soils and dead things to make food.
    (b) The process of making food in plants.
    (c) How animals rely on plants for food.
    (d) How energy passes between things.

28. Ponds and lakes represent what type of biome?
    (a) Flowing-water
    (b) Wetlands
    (c) Standing-water
    (d) Intertidal zones

29. Which of the following is/are the key features of the Indian Constitution?
    (a) Federalism
    (b) Parliamentary Form of Government
    (c) Separation of Powers
    (d) All of the above

30. What is considered as the most important symbol of the Indian Democracy?
    (a) Preamble   (b) Leader
    (c) Parliament   (d) All of these

31. Where is the seven North Eastern states have a common High Court located at?
    (a) Imphal   (b) Guwahati
    (c) Shillong   (d) Dispur

32. Myopia is corrected by using which type of lens?
    (a) Concave
    (b) Convex
    (c) Both (a) and (b)
    (d) Neither (a) nor (b)

33. What is the unit of frequency?
    (a) Hertz   (b) Volume
    (c) Decible   (d) Ampere

34. Which of the following has the largest storage capacity?
    (a) CPU   (b) DVD
    (c) Hard disk   (d) Pen Drive

35. Who was the first Indian to swim across the English Channel?
    (a) Arti Shah   (b) Mihir Sen
    (c) Sushil Kumar   (d) Baldev Singh

36. The first city of India to have an e-court is………. .
    (a) Ahmedabad   (b) Delhi
    (c) Uttar Pradesh   (d) Andhra Pradesh

37. Who was the first Indian Commander-in-chief of free India?
    (a) Arjan Singh   (b) K.M. Cariappa
    (c) Anjali Gupta   (d) S.S Tigga

38. South Asian Association for Regional Cooperation (SAARC) has its headquarter in …… .
    (a) Delhi   (b) Beijing
    (c) Kathmandu   (d) Dhaka

39. The terms Volley, Smash, Service are related to which among the following sports?
    (a) Volleyball   (b) Lawn Tennis
    (c) Table Tennis   (d) Badminton

40. World Health Organisation (WHO) has designated 2020 as ………. .
    (a) International Year of Sustainable Tourism for Development
    (b) International Year of Light and Light-based Technologies
    (c) International Year of Nurse and Midwife
    (d) None of the above

2 Marks Questions

41. Which of the following statements regarding how did the British conquer India and establish their rule is not correct?

(a) They subjugated local Nawabs and Rajas.

(b) They brought changes in rulers and tastes, customs and practices.

(c) They established control over the economy and collected revenue to meet all their expenses.

(d) None of the above

42. Which of the following is not a correct statement?

(a) Jarawa tribe is native of Andaman Nicobar Islands.

(b) There is no presence of tribal population on Lakshadweep Islands.

(c) Jharkhand has maximum tribal population in India.

(d) Sixth Schedule of Indian Constitution deals with the Scheduled and Tribal Areas.

43. Which of the following was not the main cause of sepoy mutiny of 1857?

(a) The policy of annexation by Britishers made Indians furious.

(b) The continuous interference of English in the basic way of living, traditional beliefs, values and norms.

(c) The Sepoys were convinced that the English were conspiring to convert them to Christianity.

(d) The Sepoys were forced to sign an agreement of debt with Britishers.

44. Which of the following statement is correct?

1. The Non-Cooperation Movement started by Gandhiji led to India's Independence form British rule.

2. The Salt Law was broken by Gandhiji during Civil Disobedience Movement.

Codes

(a) Only 1   (b) Only 2

(c) Both 1 and 2   (d) None of these

45. Consider the following statements about Biosphere reserves.

1. Biosphere Reserves are areas of terrestrial and coastal ecosystems but not part of UNESCO.

2. These reserves are rich in biodiversity and cultural heritage.

Which of the statements given above is/are correct?

(a) Only 1

(b) Only 2

(c) Both 1 and 2

(d) Neither 1 nor 2

46. Which of the following is not an advantage of mixed cropping?

(a) Greater stability of yield over different seasons.

(b) One crop may provide physical support to another one.

(c) Better control of weeds, pests, and diseases.

(d) Helps in rising underground water.

47. Consider the following statements.

1. Plants absorb Carbon Dioxide from the atmosphere for photosynthesis.

2. Deforestation results in decreased number of trees leading to accumulation of Carbon Dioxide in the atmosphere.

3. Carbon Dioxide in the atmosphere traps heat rays reflected by the Earth which results in Global Warming.

Which of the above statements is/are true regarding how deforestation is associated with global warming?
(a) Both 1 and 3   (b) Both 2 and 3
(c) Only 2   (d) All of these

48. Which of the following did not include in the highlights of the text prepared by Dr. B.R. Ambedkar, who was the Chairman of the Constitution Drafting Committee?
(a) Freedom of Religion
(b) Abolition of Untouchability
(c) Economic and Social Rights for Women
(d) Fundamental Duties

49. Which of the following statement is correct?

1. The Supreme Court is the highest court in the country.

2. The decisions made by Parliament can be reviewed by Supreme Court.

3. The Supreme Court is located in Kolkata.

Codes
(a) Only 1, 3   (b) Only 2, 3
(c) Only 1, 2   (d) All of these

50. Which of the following statement is correct?

1. A member of Parliament is directly elected to the Upper House of Parliament.

2. The Chairman of Upper House of Parliament is Vice-President.

Codes
(a) Only 1
(b) Only 2
(c) Both 1 and 2
(d) All of the above

Answers

Chapter 1   Introduction to European Power

1. (c)	2. (a)	3. (a)	4. (b)	5. (a)	6. (a)	7. (b)	8. (b)	9. (d)	10. (c)
11. (a)	12. (d)	13. (c)	14. (b)	15. (c)	16. (d)	17. (b)	18. (c)	19. (a)	

Chapter 2   Tribal Movement

1. (a)	2. (c)	3. (d)	4. (c)	5. (c)	6. (c)	7. (a)	8. (c)	9. (c)	10. (b)
11. (c)	12. (a)	13. (c)	14. (a)	15. (b)	16. (c)	17. (a)	18. (b)	19. (d)	20. (a)
21. (c)									

Chapter 3   Revolt of 1857

1. (a)	2. (a)	3. (b)	4. (c)	5. (a)	6. (b)	7. (c)	8. (c)	9. (a)	10. (c)
11. (a)	12. (c)	13. (a)	14. (c)	15. (a)	16. (d)	17. (b)	18. (d)	19. (d)	20. (b)
21. (c)									

Chapter 4   Women, Caste and Reforms

1. (b)	2. (d)	3. (b)	4. (b)	5. (a)	6. (c)	7. (b)	8. (b)	9. (c)	10. (a)
11. (a)	12. (b)	13. (a)	14. (c)	15. (c)	16. (c)	17. (b)			

Chapter 5   National Movement of India

1. (d)	2. (c)	3. (b)	4. (d)	5. (d)	6. (c)	7. (a)	8. (a)	9. (c)	10. (a)
11. (c)	12. (c)	13. (d)	14. (a)	15. (c)	16. (a)	17. (c)	18. (a)	19. (b)	20. (b)
21. (c)	22. (a)	23. (a)	24. (d)	25. (c)	26. (c)	27. (a)	28. (a)	29. (c)	30. (a)
31. (c)	32. (b)								

Chapter 6   India After Independence

1. (b)	2. (b)	3. (d)	4. (c)	5. (d)	6. (c)	7. (a)	8. (b)	9. (c)	10. (b)
11. (d)	12. (d)	13. (c)	14. (d)	15. (c)	16. (c)	17. (c)	18. (a)	19. (c)	20. (c)

Chapter 7   Land, Soil and Water Resources

1. (d)	2. (c)	3. (b)	4. (b)	5. (a)	6. (d)	7. (a)	8. (d)	9. (d)	10. (d)
11. (c)	12. (c)	13. (c)	14. (a)	15. (c)	16. (d)	17. (c)	18. (c)	19. (c)	20. (c)
21. (c)	22. (d)	23. (d)	24. (c)	25. (b)	26. (c)	27. (c)	28. (a)	29. (c)	

Chapter 8   Natural Vegetation and Wildlife

1. (d)	2. (c)	3. (d)	4. (b)	5. (c)	6. (a)	7. (c)	8. (d)	9. (b)	10. (b)
11. (a)	12. (d)	13. (a)	14. (a)	15. (c)	16. (a)	17. (a)	18. (d)	19. (d)	20. (c)
21. (a)									

Chapter 9   Minerals and Power Resources

1.	(d)	2.	(c)	3.	(a)	4.	(d)	5.	(d)	6.	(c)	7.	(b)	8.	(c)	9.	(a)	10.	(b)
11.	(c)	12.	(b)	13.	(b)	14.	(d)	15.	(c)	16.	(a)	17.	(d)	18.	(b)	19.	(b)	20.	(d)
21.	(a)	22.	(d)																	

Chapter 10   Agriculture

1.	(b)	2.	(c)	3.	(c)	4.	(a)	5.	(b)	6.	(c)	7.	(a)	8.	(b)	9.	(d)	10.	(b)
11.	(b)	12.	(c)	13.	(c)	14.	(d)	15.	(a)	16.	(d)	17.	(c)	18.	(b)	19.	(a)		

Chapter 11   Industries

1.	(a)	2.	(a)	3.	(d)	4.	(b)	5.	(c)	6.	(a)	7.	(a)	8.	(c)	9.	(c)	10.	(a)
11.	(c)	12.	(a)	13.	(b)	14.	(b)	15.	(d)	16.	(b)	17.	(b)						

Chapter 12   Human Resource (Population)

1.	(a)	2.	(c)	3.	(a)	4.	(c)	5.	(b)	6.	(b)	7.	(d)	8.	(a)	9.	(d)	10.	(c)
11.	(c)	12.	(a)	13.	(c)														

Chapter 13   Ecology and Environment

1.	(a)	2.	(a)	3.	(d)	4.	(a)	5.	(c)	6.	(b)	7.	(a)	8.	(b)	9.	(a)	10.	(b)
11.	(d)	12.	(b)	13.	(c)	14.	(c)	15.	(d)	16.	(a)	17.	(b)	18.	(d)	19.	(d)	20.	(c)
21.	(b)																		

Chapter 14   Indian Constitution

1.	(b)	2.	(c)	3.	(b)	4.	(d)	5.	(c)	6.	(b)	7.	(a)	8.	(a)	9.	(c)	10.	(c)
11.	(a)	12.	(a)	13.	(b)	14.	(c)	15.	(a)								

Chapter 15   Our Parliament

1.	(a)	2.	(b)	3.	(d)	4.	(b)	5.	(b)	6.	(c)	7.	(b)	8.	(b)	9.	(c)	10.	(d)
11.	(b)	12.	(c)	13.	(c)	14.	(c)	15.	(c)	16.	(c)	17.	(a)						

Chapter 16   Our Judiciary

1.	(a)	2.	(c)	3.	(b)	4.	(c)	5.	(a)	6.	(a)	7.	(c)	8.	(c)	9.	(d)	10.	(a)
11.	(b)	12.	(d)	13.	(b)	14.	(c)	15.	(b)	16.	(d)	17.	(b)	18.	(a)				

Chapter 17   Science and Technology

1.	(a)	2.	(c)	3.	(d)	4.	(b)	5.	(b)	6.	(b)	7.	(c)	8.	(b)	9.	(a)	10.	(d)
11.	(b)	12.	(b)	13.	(d)	14.	(a)	15.	(b)	16.	(c)	17.	(c)	18.	(b)	19.	(c)	20.	(d)
21.	(d)	22.	(c)	23.	(a)	24.	(b)	25.	(a)	26.	(b)	27.	(a)	28.	(b)	29.	(c)		

Chapter 18   Computers

1. (b)	**2.** (b)	**3.** (a)	**4.** (d)	**5.** (a)	**6.** (d)	**7.** (a)	**8.** (b)	**9.** (c)	**10.** (a)
11. (c)	**12.** (a)	**13.** (b)	**14.** (c)	**15.** (d)	**16.** (b)	**17.** (a)	**18.** (a)	**19.** (d)	**20.** (b)

Chapter 19   General Knowledge

1. (a)	**2.** (c)	**3.** (b)	**4.** (a)	**5.** (b)	**6.** (c)	**7.** (b)	**8.** (c)	**9.** (a)	**10.** (b)
11. (c)	**12.** (d)	**13.** (a)	**14.** (b)	**15.** (c)	**16.** (b)	**17.** (c)	**18.** (a)	**19.** (d)	**20.** (b)
21. (c)									

Chapter 20   Defence

1. (a)	**2.** (b)	**3.** (d)	**4.** (a)	**5.** (d)	**6.** (b)	**7.** (a)	**8.** (a)	**9.** (c)	**10.** (d)
11. (a)	**12.** (c)	**13.** (b)	**14.** (a)	**15.** (c)	**16.** (d)				

Chapter 21   International Organisation

1. (b)	**2.** (c)	**3.** (a)	**4.** (c)	**5.** (c)	**6.** (c)	**7.** (c)	**8.** (a)	**9.** (b)	**10.** (b)
11. (a)	**12.** (b)	**13.** (c)	**14.** (a)	**15.** (c)	**16.** (d)	**17.** (c)			

Chapter 22   Sports

1. (c)	**2.** (a)	**3.** (b)	**4.** (c)	**5.** (a)	**6.** (d)	**7.** (d)	**8.** (c)	**9.** (b)	**10.** (b)
11. (b)	**12.** (c)	**13.** (b)	**14.** (a)	**15.** (c)	**16.** (c)	**17.** (b)	**18.** (a)	**19.** (d)	**20.** (b)
21. (d)	**22.** (a)	**23.** (a)							

Practice Set 1

1. (b)	**2.** (b)	**3.** (c)	**4.** (a)	**5.** (c)	**6.** (a)	**7.** (a)	**8.** (b)	**9.** (c)	**10.** (d)
11. (b)	**12.** (a)	**13.** (a)	**14.** (b)	**15.** (c)	**16.** (c)	**17.** (a)	**18.** (b)	**19.** (d)	**20.** (a)
21. (c)	**22.** (b)	**23.** (c)	**24.** (c)	**25.** (c)	**26.** (b)	**27.** (b)	**28.** (c)	**29.** (a)	**30.** (a)
31. (d)	**32.** (a)	**33.** (b)	**34.** (a)	**35.** (b)	**36.** (b)	**37.** (a)	**38.** (d)	**39.** (c)	**40.** (a)
41. (c)	**42.** (a)	**43.** (a)	**44.** (c)	**45.** (b)	**46.** (c)	**47.** (c)	**48.** (c)	**49.** (a)	**50.** (a)

Practice Set 2

1. (b)	**2.** (b)	**3.** (a)	**4.** (c)	**5.** (d)	**6.** (c)	**7.** (b)	**8.** (c)	**9.** (a)	**10.** (b)
11. (a)	**12.** (c)	**13.** (b)	**14.** (a)	**15.** (a)	**16.** (a)	**17.** (d)	**18.** (c)	**19.** (b)	**20.** (c)
21. (d)	**22.** (a)	**23.** (c)	**24.** (b)	**25.** (d)	**26.** (b)	**27.** (b)	**28.** (b)	**29.** (d)	**30.** (c)
31. (b)	**32.** (a)	**33.** (a)	**34.** (c)	**35.** (b)	**36.** (a)	**37.** (b)	**38.** (c)	**39.** (b)	**40.** (c)
41. (d)	**42.** (c)	**43.** (d)	**44.** (b)	**45.** (b)	**46.** (d)	**47.** (d)	**48.** (d)	**49.** (c)	**50.** (b)